Come By Here

Come By Here

A Memoir *in* Essays *from* Georgia's Geechee Coast

Neesha Powell-Ingabire

HUB CITY PRESS
SPARTANBURG, SC

Cover design: Meg Reid

Interior book design: Kate McMullen

Photography: Keamber Pearson, Aimée-Josiane
Powell-Ingabire, Neesha Powell-Ingabire

Proofreaders: Melissa Thorpe, Tanaya Winder

This essay collection is a work of creative nonfiction, written to the best of the author's memory.
Some names and identifying details have been
changed to respect the privacy of the people
involved, and some dialogue has been recreated.

Library of Congress
Cataloging-in-Publication Data

Powell-Ingabire, Denechia, 1987- author.
Come by here : a memoir in essays from Georgia's
Geechee Coast / Neesha Powell-Ingabire.
Other titles: Memoir in essays from Georgia's Geechee
Coast
Description: Spartanburg, SC : Hub City Press, [2024]
Identifiers:
    LCCN 2024011620 (print)
    LCCN 2024011621 (ebook)
    ISBN 9798885740388 (trade paperback)
    ISBN 9798885740432 (epub)
Subjects:
    LCSH: Powell-Ingabire, Denechia, 1987-
    African Americans–Georgia–Brunswick–Biography.
    Brunswick (Ga.)–Race relations–History–21st century.
    Brunswick (Ga.)–Biography.
    Gullahs–Social life and customs.
Classification:
LCC F294.B9 P68 2024 (print)
LCC F294.B9 (ebook)
DDC 975.8/742092 [B]–dc23/eng/20240327

LC record available at https://lccn.loc.gov/2024011620

HUB CITY PRESS
200 Ezell Street
Spartanburg, SC 29306
864.577.9349 | www.hubcity.org

For Mommy, Grandma, Mother, and Aimée-Josiane—
there would be no book without y'all.

Contents

Who has the rights to the story of a place? Are these rights earned, bought, fought and died for? Or are they given? Are they automatic, like an assumption? Self-renewing?

Are these rights a token of citizenship belonging to those who stay in the place or to those who leave and come back to it? Does the act of leaving relinquish one's rights to the story of a place? Who stays gone? Who can afford to return?

SARAH M. BROOM, *THE YELLOW HOUSE* (2019)

My own story has meaning only as long as it is a part of the overall story of my people.

WILMA MANKILLER

I.
Kindred

Entrance of the St. Simons Island Pier, St. Simons, Georgia.

Hometown Memories

EATING CHICKEN TENDERS AND POTATO SPUDS AT Spanky's by the mall or by the marsh on Highway 17 for special occasions. The rumor our town might get a Red Lobster one day. Seeing Grandma working every day in my elementary school cafeteria. When she told me the Black cafeteria workers cheered because O.J. won his case. Riding from Altama Elementary School (go Eagles!) to Grandma's apartment in her smoky white sedan. Sitting on the handlebars of my sister Nicole's bike to explore "Bumpy Road" in a nearby trailer park. Mama forbidding us to ever go back to Bumpy Road. The time we stood outside of Mandy and Rhiannon's house and heard their mom call us "niggers." Stumbling around on the floor of Skateland 17 to thumping beats by Puff Daddy and slow jams by Usher. Friday nights were for white kids, Saturday nights for Black.

The cow on top of the Nick's Country Buffet sign across from the skating rink. Pinching my nose on the school bus riding past the rotting garbage smell downtown. Lye relaxer burning my scalp in a hair salon on Altama Avenue. Hanging out at Walmart with all the other teenagers. Driving around aimlessly out of boredom. Cheering Friday nights on the sidelines for Brunswick High. Sonic after Friday night football games. Working the register at Pablo's Mexican Restaurant on Saturday mornings with a raspy voice. Paying thirty-five cents at the toll on the St. Simons Island causeway. The week of high school graduation, partying in a rental house on East Beach where rich people lived. Paying my share for the beach house with Pizza Hut earnings. Underage drinking Skyy Blue, Smirnoff Ice, and Hypnotiq. Making out on the St. Simons pier. Posing on the sculpture of a mama and baby whale at the pier. Laughing at drunks and tourists at the pier. Spending too much damn time at the pier because life feels less mundane when you're standing beside the ocean. Pointing to the lighthouse a few steps away from the pier and telling whoever's with me, "A woman killed herself by jumping from the top." Sitting on a rock wall protecting the land from the water. Wondering what lie on the other side.

Neesha and Grandma at Neesha's high school graduation, 2005.

Finding Grandma

"YOU KNOW I CAN DINE WITH KINGS AND QUEENS," Grandma said to me, a glint in her eye. She invoked this saying whenever we were in an atmosphere we considered fancy. The last time I remember her saying it, we were eating breakfast at a University of Georgia (UGA) Parents Weekend, sitting underneath a big white tent with my mother and my boyfriend alongside other families. This was Grandma's first and final visit to my college. We sat on the lawn beside the campus chapel, an imposing white Greek Revival structure with six huge columns. I remember a Black administrator making a point to come over and shake our hands. I hoped he could sense what an upstanding person Grandma was. I felt proud to show her off and to show her how far I had come since being that little girl with pink bifocals going through my school's lunch line, waving at her bustling in the kitchen.

Mama hadn't seen me since dropping me off at school a few months before. She did what she often did while sitting across from me: pick me apart. In an attempt to dodge her criticism, I had tried to look as presentable as possible for her visit. Hair freshly relaxed and growing bangs pulled back with a beaded bobby pin, I wore a Gap shirt, dress pants, and ballerina flats. As I scooped scrambled eggs into my mouth, Mama remarked on my top lip being darker than my bottom, as if I hadn't had the same lips since birth.

"Why do they look like that?" she asked, as if they were abnormal.

Her words burst the balloon of confidence I had built up since being on my own since August. I was excelling in my classes, making new friends, doing what I liked when I liked for the very first time. But now my attention was being diverted to the miscoloring of my lips by the very person who created them.

"That's the beauty in it," Grandma calmly explained to Mama.

I smiled and returned to my food. Grandma had my back like always. She looked at me with love in her eyes when Mama looked at me with disdain. She made me feel like I could do no wrong. She let her daughter know not only were my lips perfectly fine, but they were a marvel. I believed her perspective over Mama's because I saw her as an authority on beauty.

After breakfast, we went to a welcome event at the chapel. We sat on the main floor in red upholstered chairs encircled by balconies, facing a stage adorned with one of the world's largest oil paintings, a depiction of the ornate interior of St. Peter's Basilica in Vatican City. It's easy to understand why Grandma felt regal there. Declaring she had what it took to dine with royalty was her way of asserting although she never attended college, she conducted herself with as much class, style, and sophistication as any PhD in our company.

Grandma introduced me to the concept of glamor. Each Christmas, she gifted me and my sister, Nicole, with a Holiday Barbie. A new one came out every year. They donned long, thick, coiffed hair and sparkling, shiny gowns. Black Holiday Barbies were more difficult to find than white ones in the 1990s, but Grandma always managed to secure them. We played with them when we were really little but kept them in their original packaging on our bookshelf when we got older. They were some of my most valued and valuable treasures. Mama said they might be worth a lot of money one day. Popular media led me to believe white women were the epitome of beauty, but my Holiday Barbies proved otherwise. I wanted to look like these dolls when I grew up, even though this seemed unlikely when I compared myself to them. My hair was short and thinning, while theirs was luxurious and abundant. They stood straight with their shoulders back, while I hunched over, trying to make myself shorter and less noticeable.

Looking at Grandma, I carried a kernel of hope I might grow up to be beautiful. She displayed portraits in her home where she actually looked like a Barbie. In one of my favorites, she stands in front of her apartment, leaning on a porch post, lips slightly parted, chin up, red clutch in hand, hair feathered, body shaped like a slim hourglass. She wears gold jewelry and a formfitting black dress with leg-of-mutton sleeves. At the time of the photo, she lived in a low-income apartment, yet she looks like she could fit in at a high-priced gala. Her air of regality belied her humility and quirks. She cackled when she laughed, loud and unapologetic. She chain smoked Virginia Slims and tried to conceal the smell with White Diamonds perfume. She guzzled Pepsi like it was water. She cooked a flavorful dinner for us nearly every night but rarely took a bite because she ate like a bird. Instead of buying new clothes, she sifted through me and my sisters' bags of clothes headed to Goodwill.

Grandma showed me how to be beautiful from the inside out.

Juneteenth weekend, in 2020, my spouse, Jojo, and I vacationed in Jekyll Island, where Grandma spent some of her happiest times. It was Jojo's first time there. Jekyll is about an hour from where Grandma grew up and just across the bridge from where I grew up in Brunswick. I can feel Grandma's presence on the island. As we drove onto Jekyll after paying an eight dollar parking fee, I recounted my scattered memories of the place: going to Summer Waves Water Park for free because my friends worked there, competing in dance competitions at the convention center, staying up all night talking to my boyfriend on a Days Inn landline while at cheerleading camp. I asked my spouse to accompany me to one of Grandma's favorite places: St. Andrews Beach.

When my family drove the stretch of beach on South Beachview Drive, Grandma often said matter-of-factly, "That's the only beach us Black folks could go to back in the day." In recent years, I learned one of the last slave ships in the United States illegally landed on the shores of St. Andrews Beach in 1858. Today, there's an exhibit there named after the vessel, the Wanderer Memory Trail. The beach, one of the few on the East Coast where Black people could go in the 1950s and 1960s, offered Grandma a reprieve from her daily grind and gave her a front row seat to musical giants like James Brown at the Black-owned Dolphin Club Lounge & Restaurant.

Pulling into the crowded parking lot of St. Andrews Beach, we observed people of all hues enjoying themselves. Picnicking and playing volleyball under ancient, mossy live oak trees. Watching birds from an observatory tower. Wading into the murky water. We decided to walk the memory trail first, where we were soon joined by a group of Black folks with their cameras around their necks. The trail comprises markers and music telling the story of a fictional boy named Umwalla to represent the Africans smuggled from the Congo and brought to the shores of Jekyll fifty-one years after the ban of the slave trade. I read the list of the four hundred nine surviving West African passengers that arrived on the Wanderer as if I might recognize a family name or surname. Sorrow welled up in my throat as I silently mourned the names of my ancestors lost in the Middle Passage. The names of ancestors I know are precious to me, like Augusta, my Grandma's name.

A sign on the beach cautioned against going into the water due to high bacteria levels—and we promptly ignored it. We stripped down to our bathing suits and dipped ourselves in the ocean after completing the trail. Dozens of others were in the water. We distanced ourselves from them, wanting to be in our own little world. It didn't seem like a good idea to go in deep, so we spent our time taking pictures of each other. One of my sister's memories flashed in my head. "I remember before you were born, Grandma used to take me to the beach. She would just sit back and float," Renee told me in a dreamy voice during a family vacation. "She looked *so* beautiful."

Perhaps by the time I came around, ten years after Renee, she thought herself too old to get in the water. I never got to see Grandma float.

Raised by an uncle and aunt, John Henry and Ida Mae Ford, in an all-Black hamlet called Meridian on Georgia's coast, Grandma was one of the first in her family to graduate high school (segregated, of course). After birthing my mother and my uncle Roy, she was kicked out of her church, a place that had been home, deemed unfit as an unwed teenage mother. She earned a pittance heading shrimp at the Meridian

Dock, working as a short order cook, and cleaning white people's homes, supplementing meals with seafood caught by neighbors.

Leaving her kids with her mother, she migrated to New York City in the 1960s, where she found better-paying work as a nursing assistant at a hospital after earning a certification. She arrived in her twenties—alone as far as I know—but relatives eventually joined her, including my mother when she reached her early teen years. Before then, Mama and Uncle Roy had been living with their grandmother in Darien (right next to Meridian). Uncle Roy visited his family in the Bronx but never lived there. After graduating high school, he joined the Army and found a wife in Germany. Meanwhile, seventeen and pregnant, Mama got married in Grandma's Bronx apartment to a hometown boy whose family had also migrated. Soon after came my sister, Renee, and then a divorce. With some community college under her belt, Mama met my dad on the job at Bronx State, a mental hospital. Their marriage produced my sister, Nicole, and then three years later, me.

My parents were headed to divorce by the time I was born. Mama had relocated back south to Brunswick with Grandma who could no longer find work in NYC. Mama needed a fresh start. Plus the city's HIV/AIDS and crack cocaine crises were hitting too close to home, affecting their family and friends. The two women had grown to be more like close friends than mother and daughter, with Mama calling Grandma by her first name. They would sometimes butt heads but held a sense of responsibility to one another. That's how they ended up moving home together.

A talented cook, Grandma took a job in the cafeteria of the elementary school my siblings and I attended. She lived in a few different working-class apartment buildings, from where her magical fingers grew various plants (including cannabis); whipped up low country boils with crab, shrimp, corn on the cob, sausage, potatoes, and plenty of seasoning; and kept a goldfish alive longer than I've ever seen since. She made everyone feel worthy of praise. She established a monthly birthday celebration at our church where members brought cakes and other treats for their loved ones' birthdays to eat in the annex after worship service ended. When it was your birthday, you could count on being showered with kind words you wouldn't have received otherwise, which meant a lot to an awkward, alienated child like me. Grandma wanted each member to feel recognized and respected, despite having been kicked out of that same congregation all those years before. She rejoined the church during my childhood, forgiving them for making her feel less than, exhibiting the grace of a queen.

Grandma wanted to give us grandkids the world. I cherished our one-on-one time. Driving me to her place after school in her red-striped white Pontiac Grand Prix, she would sometimes stop at Food Lion, grin in my direction, and ask, "You want a piece of candy?" Of course I did; I had an insatiable sweet tooth. She handed me her book of food stamps and pulled out a cigarette as I rushed into the grocery store. After making my selection, usually Skittles or Starbursts, I happily presented a food stamp coupon to the cashier. On those days, I felt like the luckiest granddaughter in the world. Other times, we headed to a gas station after school, and she instructed me to choose six numbers so she could play the lottery. I imagined her winning, then building a lovely home in Meridian (nothing too excessive because that wasn't her style), and handing cards filled with cash to her children and grandchildren on holidays. She'd never have to work again. I knew if her lottery numbers ever hit, our entire family would be taken care of…but they never did.

By the time I went to study journalism at UGA, Grandma had retired from her cafeteria job and lived off a small amount of money from her Social Security check and a part-time job at a convenience store. I remember when she called me during a dance practice, and I took a break to chat with her. "I miss you," she told me. "I wanna be able to send you a lil' cash." She died less than a year later, never able to send me money at school, but I know she would have if she had it.

Every pew was filled at her funeral. Dressed in black with sunglasses on, my sisters and I stood at the front of our church beside her casket as the service began, and funeral goers got their last look at her body. The moment felt so surreal that I remained composed when the funeral director closed Grandma's casket as Renee and Nicole bawled. My voice cracked but I didn't cry as I read an original poem for Grandma at the behest of Mama during the service, nor when her body was lowered into the ground at a cemetery down the street from the church in sweltering July heat.

When I returned to school the next month, I taped a photo to my wall of her holding me as a baby with her eyes turned downward and her smooth, buttery brown skin shining, accented by a red tank top and gold earrings. A year of heartbreak ensued, as I found it increasingly difficult to juggle a full class load, a part-time job, and emergent health problems—breathing issues, body aches, tingling hands, and mystery rashes. The university health center couldn't figure out what was wrong with me, so I went down Google rabbit holes for clues. I started to believe my symptoms were psychosomatic. Maybe grief and loss were manifesting in my body as illness. I no longer had a grandmother to turn to. No more of Grandma's effortless dishes. No more Holiday Barbies. No more Grandma to point at me proudly and proclaim to whoever I was one of her "grands," nor to defend me from Mama's petty judgments.

I had lost one of my biggest advocates. Mama often accused me of being a "smartass" for talking back to her, dared me to call child protective services, and threatened to kick me out. "You'll have to go live in a shelter," she would say. Her version of kicking me out was dropping me off at Grandma's and picking me up the next day. When I showed up to Grandma's apartment in tears, she would soothe me, tell me everything would be okay, and make me a plate of good food. She made me feel like I wasn't the awful kid Mama sometimes treated me like. She nurtured me in a way Mama couldn't.

Grandma gave me what she hadn't been able to give Mama. While Grandma was up north, her mother raised my mother with a switch in her hand and little affection. Mama hadn't known comfort; she'd only known beatings. I never had to worry about cooking for myself, while Mama was cooking her own meals in elementary school. Being raised without her mother gave Mama a hard edge, I think. Grandma made up for her absence in those days by showering us grands with the hugs and love my mother never got. Not only was she my reprieve from Mama but also from classmates who teased me for being cross-eyed due to strabismus (a misalignment of the eyes), my monotone voice, and a slight speech impediment in which "the" sounded like "dee." Grandma laughed at my sarcastic jokes (one of my coping mechanisms) and said I could be a model one day. She was my safe haven. Nowadays I wish I could dial her number when my mother and I bump heads or when others try to make me feel small. I remind myself I matter because I was made in her image—that I am because she was.

I never thought about visiting Grandma's gravesite until more than a decade after her death. I honored her from wherever I was. I preserved her through pictures. I posted photos of her on social media to stamp her into time immemorial. Jojo and I placed a picture of her posing with her hands on her hips front and center at our wedding reception and then on the fridge of the first home we owned (her best friends were a lesbian couple, so she wouldn't have batted an eye at two women getting married).

The photo that once graced my college apartment now sits on a bookcase turned altar tended to by me and my wife, beside photos and symbols of others we have loved and lost. This includes pictures of my wife's cousin who died during an act of senseless violence before he was even legal to drink and my wife's friend, a mother who died by suicide; the name of Jojo's deceased grandmother, Peruth, in a heart-shaped frame; my Aunt Nettie's obituary; and a tuft of our deceased dog Lev's hair. Pictures sit among stones with special meanings, figurines from Rwanda, where Jojo is from, cotton picked by a friend in Nigeria, incense, and more. At times, we've covered our altar with African wax print fabric. Jojo introduced me to the practice of keeping an altar to honor our ancestors back when we first got together in 2012. I was familiar with church altars, but I'd never known anyone with an ancestral altar.

My love for Jojo pushes me to embrace the "woo-woo," the unknown, the other side. We don't police what the other puts on our altar, as long as it pleases the ancestors. Our altar reminds me Grandma will never truly be gone as long as I carry her in my heart. I channel my grief over her death into it. I gave away most of my Holiday Barbies to the daughters of friends, but one of them has a place of honor in my office. She wears an updo and a blingy black gown, a hot pink shawl, and a crown. I keep her protected in a case.

I finally thought about Grandma's final resting place some time in 2019 when Mama called me with a proposal from Uncle Roy. He wanted our family to put a headstone on Grandma's grave and then eat at a nearby seafood restaurant. My mother loved her mother dearly; her grief is palpable when she says holidays aren't the same without Grandma. Yet, she wasn't at all amenable to her brother's suggestion.

"The family doesn't come together like that anymore," Mama said, exasperated, after informing me of Uncle Roy's plan.

Like all families, we fight, and Mama lets go of grudges at a snail's pace (we once got into a blowout after I didn't tell her about a birthday vacation to Los Angeles, resulting in us not speaking for a year). She refused to consider my uncle's plan on account of her feud with one of my sisters at the time. Our call quickly devolved into a shouting match. I hung up so infuriated by Mama's stubbornness the reality of Grandma's unmarked grave barely registered. I hadn't been to her grave since her funeral, so I always assumed she had a headstone.

For fourteen years, I neglected to visit Grandma's grave because my relationship with home is complicated. It's difficult to separate my feelings about coastal Georgia from my childhood of being bullied for looking and talking funny, perpetually being one of the only Black kids in "gifted" classes, and being called "nigger" by a stranger in the school cafeteria. I spent years avoiding my hometown and even moved clear across the country with Jojo to Seattle in 2014. After four years, we moved back south and settled in Atlanta, five hours away from my hometown. Despite being closer to home, I had no intention of visiting initially. It took a tremendous loss in my home community for me to return.

The COVID-19 pandemic had just begun when I came across a *New York Times* article one afternoon about the murder of Ahmaud Arbery, a Black man shot and killed while jogging in a Brunswick subdivision by three white men. Seeing the name and photo of the man who pulled the trigger, Travis McMichael, felt like a punch to the gut: The eyes of a redheaded man who as a boy wore hunting jackets and Confederate flags in our shared high school Spanish class stared back at me. I never paid attention to the guy because I (correctly) assumed he was racist. A few days later, over the phone, my little brother told me Ahmaud's football locker was near his own in high school. A video of Ahmaud being gunned down and left to die on the ground went viral soon after the *New York Times* story came out. It felt like a surreal nightmare as it circulated around the world.

My heart ached for this twenty-five-year-old man I never knew but could've easily been my own brother, his family, his friends, and every Black person in Brunswick. Despite always feeling like an outsider there, I still considered it home. I cared about it because Grandma cared about it. I imagined her listening to the news of the murder on her car radio, taking a drag of her cigarette, and lamenting, "Jesus wept as the disciples prayed." Her signature saying for when things were a damn shame. I couldn't help but grieve this tragedy in my hometown, where most of my memories with Grandma take place. Then I couldn't help but feel proud seeing the community rally to win justice for Ahmaud. I had never seen my town go so hard. I wanted to be part of ensuring there is never another case in Brunswick as heinous as Ahmaud's. Already freelancing as a journalist, I began reporting on the uprisings spurred by Ahmaud's death, including the victorious moment when the three perpetrators received guilty verdicts. Grandma used to say I would grow up to be rich and successful. I'm still working on the rich part, but I know Grandma would consider my writing a success. She looks over my shoulder as I bang on my laptop keyboard.

Now I immerse myself in parts of my hometown's history I never learned in school, clueing me into why it is the way it is and why I experienced it the way I did. I always knew Black people there were systematically oppressed because Black people across the diaspora are systematically oppressed, but I never knew the depths of their specific oppressions. Black folks indigenous to Georgia's coast have been recovering and sharing their ancestors' stories for decades, like Cornelia Walker Bailey (1945-2017), the former unofficial griot or storyteller of Sapelo Island who wrote the memoir *God, Dr. Buzzard, and the Bolito Man: A Saltwater Geechee Talks About Life on Sapelo Island, Georgia* (2001), and the Geechee Gullah Ring Shouters of McIntosh County. Yet their work is seldom amplified nor incorporated into textbooks, especially in our current age where "woke" curriculum is being attacked, thus Black kids in coastal Georgia grow up feeling like outsiders.

A lot of us feel compelled to run away, ignorant of our rich history.

After nearly a decade of avoiding home, now my spouse tells me I get excited when we get off the highway exit to Brunswick. My face lights up with familiarity as I point out all my old haunts.

As a child, my siblings and I, Mama, and Grandma drove every Sunday from Brunswick to church in Meridian. I found these drives to be sleepy and dull, all blue skies and marshes with few signs of human life (a scenic drive in retrospect). Maybe I would've thought differently if I'd known about the blood, sweat, and tears embedded in every mile of the trip. Only in the past few years did I find out the dilapidated white mansion sitting on top of wetlands on Highway 17 was built on Butler Island Plantation where enslaved Africans once cultivated rice. A tall brick structure in front of the mansion remains from when a rice mill operated there. Some of the enslaved Africans on the plantation were sold by Pierce Mease Butler in the largest slave auction in history, now known as the "Weeping Time" because of the rain pouring down during the travesty (their descendants are now fighting to save the property from speculative developers).

If my family elders knew these stories, they never talked about them. I can understand how they might've evoked shame and inferiority. But I'm part of a generation of Black creators who seek to remove the stigma of descending from enslaved Africans. I want to help preserve ancestral stories for those who come after me, including my niblings, little cousins, and future children. I want them to know where to find themselves.

Heading home from me and my spouse's Juneteenth vacation to Jekyll, I decided to take the scenic route to I-95 North on the country highways my family used to travel to church. First Highway 17, where we drove past Butler Island Plantation. Then Highway 99, which takes you right past my old red-roofed church and the cemetery where Grandma is buried.

I slowed down as I approached the tabby cemetery entrance and turned toward Jojo.

"I need to find Grandma."

I hadn't planned it, but it was one of my first times coming back home since my self-imposed exile. It was only right to pay my respects to the best part of home. I wanted to feel close to my grandmother during a time I was grappling with whether I belonged. Around noon, I turned onto a path in the cemetery and parked our car. Jojo and I got out, and began searching. The weather was as scorching as it had been at Grandma's funeral, and mosquitoes were feasting on our blood, but I didn't want to leave until I found her grave. There were elaborate, well-kept headstones bearing last names I remembered from church—Jordan, McIntosh, Mitchell, Palmer—but no Grandma. I became frustrated and desperate as I walked deeper into the cemetery. Why couldn't my grandmother have a headstone, too? And how the hell were we going to identify an unmarked grave?

What must have been Grandma whispering led me to a row of three graves partially hidden by shrubbery, leaves, grass, and dirt. I read the name engraved on top of the middle one: Ida Mae Ford—the aunt who raised my grandmother. I yelled to Jojo to come over and look. Pay dirt. I felt like I had finally won the lottery for Grandma.

I'm not sure whether Grandma lies to the left or right of Ida. I brushed off debris from the concrete slabs on either side of Ida's grave, trying to feel in my heart which one was her. There are tiny green markers by the graves with slips of paper in them too weathered to be legible. When I called Mama to ask about it, she didn't sound very certain.

My family couldn't afford a headstone at the time of Grandma's burial, but we can afford one now. What would I like to see carved into her headstone?

"Here lies Augusta, mother, grandmother, sister, and aunt. A beloved, beautiful, and regal soul."

Dreams Have Wings *mural by Roderrick Davis in downtown Brunswick, Georgia depicting a young Black girl holding a butterfly.*

A Treatise on Black Women's Tears

I.

"Are you always this teary?" the nurse asked as she finished extracting vials of blood from my right arm.

"No," I choked out.

If I'd been in my right state of mind, I would've been embarrassed crying in front of this white ponytailed brunette who looked to be around my age, twenty-three. But I was not myself. That morning, I'd driven from my girlfriend's apartment in Columbia, South Carolina, four hours north to Durham, North Carolina, where I served as a HIV/AIDS outreach and education AmeriCorps member earning minimum wage. The closer I got to Durham, the more disconnected from reality I felt. The raspy voice I had been hearing each night for the past few months had gotten too loud. I was confused whether the voice was internal or external, but wherever it was coming from, it wanted me dead. My failing relationship, my first one with another woman, compounded the effects of the gnawing voice. So did living away from home, Georgia, for the first time.

"I can't make it to work today," I texted my supervisor while driving.

After getting off at the exit to my apartment, I continued driving past my turn until I arrived at a parking deck at Duke University Hospital, where I'd visited in my capacity as an AmeriCorps member. I parked in a garage, crossed the street, and walked through a covered walkway for what felt like eons until I got to the emergency room front desk.

"I'm thinking about killing myself," I calmly announced to the receptionist.

She checked me in, and it didn't take long for me to be ushered to the back. A nurse took my vitals and asked me to change into a hospital gown. For a while, I sat alone underneath fluorescent lights in a cold, little cubicle with two solid walls and two curtained walls, waiting for whatever came next. As soon as the ponytailed nurse entered the room, she bombarded me with questions: Do you have a family history of mental illness? *I'm not sure.* Do you use alcohol or drugs? *Yes, I drink. I've tried marijuana a few times.* Have you attempted suicide before? *No, just thought about it…a lot.* Do you currently have a plan for killing yourself? *Not really.* Her endless queries triggered my waterworks. I cried initially because I felt overwhelmed. I kept crying because it felt cathartic. I was finally getting help after months of calling around town to schedule a therapy appointment and getting nowhere. I was so relieved that when the nurse asked if I was "always this teary," I forgot to feel ashamed.

When the nurse left, a middle-aged Black nursing assistant came to sit in my room until the doctor came. He sat with me, as we silently listened to the typical hustle and bustle of an ER, until it was disrupted by cursing and screaming. We caught a glimpse of the culprit, a disheveled, young Black woman in the hallway struggling to escape the arms of staff guiding her to a nearby cubicle. I couldn't make out exactly what she was saying, but she was irate.

"Aw, don't worry about her," the nursing assistant told me. "You know, when you get out of this place, nobody will know you were ever here. You can go back to living your normal life." To him, the woman's outbursts were abnormal. Maybe, the man couldn't reconcile her erratic behavior with the meek, quiet patient in front of him. But inside, I felt as manic as she was behaving and admired her for not showing restraint. I wondered what the nursing assistant would think if I suddenly lost my shit like her, whether he would still have kind words for me. I only seemed normal to him because my mental anguish had manifested as grief instead of rage.

The psychiatrist eventually entered my cubicle with more questions in tow.

"Do you think you need to stay here overnight?" he asked. Something in his tone felt as if he might be getting impatient with me.

"I don't know…." I replied. My eyes welled back up.

"You should stay with us for the night," the doctor decided.

I got transported to Duke Hospital's psychiatric ward in the back of a cop car. I had never been in one. The ride was quick and unremarkable. I wasn't treated harshly, probably because the cops didn't see me as a criminal. The next morning, I burst into tears as a large team of clinicians grilled me, staring me down like a lab rat. Their questions and comments barely registered because I was so overwhelmed. What I did comprehend wasn't comforting. My tears dried as I got used to life in the psych ward. I complied with taking psych meds, got used to being woken up every few hours by staff checking my vital signs. My mind finally got to rest. I had little contact with the outside world except for occasional calls on a shared landline (they took away my cell) and a visit from my roommate, and there were few responsibilities aside from participating in mandatory games and dance classes. At the end of my three-day stay, I had a prescription for psych meds and appointments scheduled with a psychiatrist and a therapist.

I left feeling hopeful, like shedding so many tears had made me lighter. Inhaling fresh air outside the hospital felt so good, I decided to give life a second chance. That meant embracing all the tears that were to come. A few weeks later when my girlfriend broke up with me, I again cried uncontrollably. I cried on the phone about it to my sister, Nicole, while squatting next to a vending machine at work. Later that year, I cried silently as I told her and Mama over the phone about my psych ward stay. I don't know how I would've gotten through that period without my tears. Each crying spell felt as if I were summoning the strength to push on.

II.

To this day, I'm cautious of wearing my heart on my sleeve, despite experiencing the usefulness of letting my emotions flow with abandon. I'm not brave enough to be a wailing woman, even though it's in my blood. During a 2021 family vacation where I prodded Mama for family lore, she told me Grandma knew how to wail.

"She learned at a funeral she went to with Jack in South Carolina," she said.

Jack is Mama's late father, Grandma's former husband whom she divorced when Mama was a little girl. I remember Grandma mentioning Jack was from a place in South Carolina that made her feel like she had gone back in time, with shacks and sharecropping, but I don't remember her mentioning wailing. She probably thought it too "old school" for me to care about. I was nineteen when she died, so I can't ask her about it. I wish she were alive so I could tell her I do care and want to know every detail. What or whom compelled her to join in on the wailing? Did it look like the scene in Toni Morrison's *Beloved* when the elderly lay minister Baby Suggs urges her congregation to weep in the woods, to cry "for the living and dead"? When I envision Grandma wailing, I feel a sense of home—like mourning out loud is a birthright that I will claim someday.

After learning of Grandma's experience in South Carolina, I became obsessed with public wailing. I wish Mama knew more about what happened. I try to imagine what it was like through research. Public wailing is an art as ancient as the Bible performed on nearly every continent at one time or another. It comforts, entertains, and can even be a career. In some cultures, the more professional mourners at a person's funeral, the more status their family has. Public wailing is typically performed by women because, of course, men aren't supposed to cry. I often encountered public wailing at church, where I would look on with curiosity. What demons were they fighting? I remember mostly women engaging in the practice. Even being in the house of their Father didn't allow men at my missionary Baptist church to feel free enough to cry out loud.

Grandma knew how to wail, yet I can't imagine Mama wailing in public. I can count on one hand the number of times I've seen my mother cry. She wore black sunglasses on the front pew of the church at her mother's funeral, so I couldn't tell if she was crying. She didn't want us kids to cry at home either. If I cried because I was sad or hurt, she would sternly ask, "What's wrong?" and attempt to solve the problem immediately. When I got in trouble and cried, she would yell, "Don't give me those crocodile tears," or "Stop crying, or I'll give you something to cry about." She acted like I never had a good reason for crying, but I cried anyway.

Crying made me feel guilty, but I couldn't control myself. I tried not to make a lot of noise when I did. I cried when other kids relentlessly made fun of my crossed eyes, speech impediment, and protruding forehead. I cried at cheerleading camp nearly every summer. My first year cheering in seventh grade, my period came on the first day of cheerleading camp, and I was unprepared. When I alerted a coach, she took me to the front office, where they gave me a tampon. I'd been wearing pads for the past year, so I could barely insert it. Toward the beginning of camp, one of the two coaches mentioned she wanted me to try out to be an all-star, but ultimately, other girls were selected to compete for the honor. I was considered for the jump-off competition, but my team ended up choosing others to represent us. We spent the night in our school gym, and my emotions were too tender to be away from home.

Heading to the showers after the first day of camp, I didn't answer when one of my only friends on the squad, a tiny Black girl who I'd met in drama club, spotted me and asked, "What's wrong?" I couldn't articulate why I was crying. I couldn't put words to my fluctuating hormones mingled with disappointment and difficulty adjusting to a new environment. Even though I'd been raised to hold my tears in and to not be weak or needy, and even though it was embarrassing to cry year after year at camp, I had to. Physiologically, I couldn't stop the tears from coming. The release always felt good, and then I would be pretty much okay for the rest of the school year.

Either silently or away from others' gaze, I cried a good deal in my adolescence. When my new girlfriend, K, helped me move to Durham in 2010, a year after I finished college, I wasn't anticipating tears. I had been accepted into an AmeriCorps program where I'd be earning poverty wages, but I thought the experience and training would be invaluable. A baby gay with a big heart, I desired a career where I could support other LGBTQIA+ people, and I thought working in the HIV/AIDS field could help me actualize this. And, I looked forward to adventure and fun in a new place...but instead found loneliness. My roommate, a fellow AmeriCorps member, was busy dating locally and applying to medical school. Flying out to interviews most weekends, she didn't have much time to socialize. I didn't know how to make friends as a grown-up (frankly I'm still figuring this out). So I visited K whenever I could in South Carolina, where we spent time with our mutual friend from high school who cooked us meals, buying ingredients with my food stamps.

I went out of my way to please K, cooking dinners (which I never did for myself), planning dates and surprises, and making her a scrapbook for Christmas. Attempting to be the perfect queer wifey, I even attended church with K when I'd rarely gone to church during college. But she never seemed as enthusiastic about our relationship as I did, more like she was just going through the motions. We had fundamental differences on issues that I felt strongly about, like abortion care: I believe abortion is a natural, normal part of life, and she didn't. Still, I was determined to make things work between us.

When I wasn't visiting K, I sat on my apartment's porch chain smoking Camel Crush cigarettes and drinking Trader Joe's wine as I mindlessly scrolled through Facebook and Twitter on my pink Chromebook. I hid being queer from most of my family because our religion and culture didn't approve. I bottled up my emotions. My appetite waned, and I dwindled from one hundred thirty-five to just under one hundred twenty pounds. At five feet and eight inches, I looked skeletal. Insomnia crept up on me at night, when the raspy voice told me what a fucked up, stupid, worthless person I was. It chanted, "I hate you, I hate you, I hate you."

The morning I drove to Duke Hospital, I woke up next to K feeling dread. My gut told me we wouldn't last much longer. Her heart wasn't in it like mine. K sent me off at the crack of dawn with a hollow kiss. Driving north on I-85, I could think of no good reason to continue living. I drove to the ER, my last resort, where I remembered how good it felt to cry in public.

III.

I have never heard a wail like that of a fellow moviegoer as I watched Tyler Perry's *For Colored Girls* (2010), an adaptation of Ntozake Shange's legendary choreopoem, *For Colored Girls Who Have Considered Suicide / When the Rainbow Is Enuf* (1976). I was on a date with K a few months before my hospitalization. The movie's main characters are all Black women who are treated badly simply for being born into the world as Black girls. A woman's husband kills her children by throwing them out of a window, another woman has a back-alley abortion, while another contracts HIV from her cheating boyfriend. These are just a few of the film's heartbreaking moments. One of these scenes evoked a piercing cry from a woman in the theater that reverberated through the air. This was no ordinary sob; it was full of mourning. I could feel it in my bones. I can only describe it as a wail. Since I was used to stifling my emotions and hadn't heard a wail like that outside of church, it startled me. I was envious of the woman's audacity to emote so loudly in public.

Dr. Manoucheka Celeste, an African American Studies professor, researches this sacred act: "Women have a long-standing and well-documented relationship with wailing and public mourning. The wailing woman is a powerful figure. In many cultures across the globe and across time, she plays an important part of community mourning and healing." In her essay, "For Crying Out Loud," novelist and African American studies professor Renee Simms dreams of a world where public wailing is more widely accepted and she could feel comfortable doing it herself: "I imagine there's freedom inside a public wail. But I can't imagine the space or occasion where it could happen, or who I would be afterward." She witnessed firsthand the communal healing power of public wailing at a family funeral where her aunt's wailing was quickly joined by other women. Simms believes the practice "disrupts the social order," and so do I. Public wailing invites communities to express their rawest emotions together in a world where we're encouraged to grieve in isolation if we want to be seen as "civilized." I wonder if making my tears more public could help me heal faster.

Celeste theorizes the reality show, *The First 48*, capitalizes off the wailing Black woman by featuring countless Black mothers grieving their murdered children. Black American tears are becoming cultural capital as TV executives, mostly white people, get rich off of them. Each week, I see so many Black mothers grieving their slain children on TV that I can't keep up with their names nor their children's names. The image of the wailing Black woman is commodified by the media every single day, when these images aren't intended for public consumption. I know folks who think transmitting photos and videos of Black death and mourning will finally convince the world Black lives matter. I've had to turn autoplay off on my social media accounts because folks post videos of Black and brown people being slaughtered, often by cops, as if it's normal to watch a human being killed. When I see these videos on TV, I change the channel.

Ever since Mamie Till-Mobley allowed photos to be taken of her son Emmett's mutilated body during the Civil Rights Movement era, all we've gotten are superficial and incremental wins. Civil rights legislation such as hate crime laws aren't enough to stop racially motivated violence from plaguing this country. Our criminal legal system is inherently illegitimate, the spawn of slave patrols and the KKK, created to police and punish Black people for simply existing. A form of chattel slavery by a different name. Our so-called justice system needs to be torn down and built anew, led by the groups most impacted by the prison industrial complex. Prisons nor the proliferation of images of Black death solve the problem of white supremacist violence. Broadcasts of Black death used to make me shed a few tears, but now they typically leave me feeling empty despair. People aren't built to grieve this much.

When videos of Tyre Nichols getting beat to death by five Memphis police officers began circulating in January 2023, I felt numb as usual. Looking at pictures of him in happier times—the tall, skinny, twenty-nine-year-old Black father, photographer, and skateboarder with Crohn's disease—reminded me of a former boyfriend; yet, I still couldn't feel anything about his murder. Then I watched Don Lemon interview his mother and stepfather, Row Vaughn and Rodney Wells, on CNN. Mrs. Wells began crying not even ten minutes in. Wearing a camel-colored dress and matching boots, tissue balled up in her hands, she described seeing her son in the early morning after his arrest and subsequent beating. Nichols' kidneys were failing, and he had gone into cardiac arrest.

"When my husband and I got to the hospital, and I saw my son, he was already gone. They had beat him to a pulp. He had bruises all over him. His head was swollen like a watermelon. His neck was busting because of the swelling. They broke his neck. My son's nose looked like an 's.' They actually just beat the crap out of him. So when I saw that, I knew my son was gone. Even if he did live, he would have been a vegetable."

Lemon commented on how a photo of Nichols in the hospital bed, taken and shared by Mr. Wells, evoked the gruesome picture of Emmett Till lying in his casket. Mrs. Wells agreed. Every time she cried, I cried. Her pain was visceral, her tears potent enough to make fellow Black women cry—even ones who have grown a protective thick skin.

All five of the police officers who beat Tyre Nichols to death were charged with a long list of crimes, including second-degree murder. All five were Black. The charges were swift, a likely attempt to protect Memphis from months-long protests, and also a clear message that Black officers won't be shielded with the same effort as their white counterparts.

Is it possible to protect the image of the wailing Black woman? Black women can start by reclaiming her for ourselves. What I mean is we should intentionally center her in our art and praxis and define the wailing Black woman on our own terms. This is what Simms and Celeste are doing, alongside a host of other artists and intellectuals, including Beyoncé. My wife and I sat in our living room transfixed during our first viewing of Beyoncé's 2016 visual album, *Lemonade*, a collage of music videos celebrating Black feminism and womanhood.

My eyes didn't well up until the visual for her song, "Forward," featuring the English singer James Blake. The tears of these Black women who will forever be associated with public wailing are now dried, and their emotions are being captured by a Southern Black woman's gaze instead of white male media executives. Blake's voice haunted me as the camera zoomed into the faces of beautifully dressed and bejeweled Black women and girls, including Sybrina Fulton, mother of

Trayvon Martin; Lezley McSpadden, mother of Mike Brown; and Gwen Carr, mother of Eric Garner. Each of the three women gets her own closeup, in which she sits holding a framed photo of her slain son as she stares into the lens with pain, dignity, and resilience in her eyes.

IV.

I think getting up in age is helping Mama see the utility of tears. Or maybe she no longer has the energy to maintain a tough façade. I last saw her cry in 2018 when we were watching Aretha Franklin's funeral on her living room TV with my wife, Jojo. The mood was more playful than sober. We laughed when the officiating pastor said he thought Ariana Grande was a new Taco Bell meal before his daughter corrected him and cringed as he groped Ariana, who was wearing her signature ponytail and a dress too sexy for your standard Black American funeral. I might've shed a tear at Chaka Khan's rendition of "Going Up Yonder," a classic gospel song performed by the church choir at Grandma's funeral, but I was too tickled at Chaka reading the lyrics off the back of her fan. I don't remember what was happening on-screen when Mama started to audibly cry. Jojo and I shot each other looks of concern. Seeing my mother cry was akin to seeing an alien ship land. I had no idea how to comfort her or if she even wanted comforting.

"What if I'm never able to see my grandkids again?" Mama moaned as she wiped her eyes.

She'd recently moved out of my sister Nicole's house. The living arrangement had run its course. I knew not seeing Nicole's kids was only the tip of the iceberg. Mama was grieving the end of an era. She became more vulnerable and mortal to me that day—no longer an impenetrable fortress. I believe she didn't cry when I was growing up because she associated it with weakness. As a single mother, she felt forced to always be the "strong Black woman." As a child, she got beaten so much that nothing could save her, especially not her tears. I never considered the source of her forever dry eyes until I got older.

Today, I know what it's like to have the strong Black woman stereotype foisted upon you, and I'm mature enough for Mama to share bits of her childhood with me. Her family was subjected to so much poverty and racism they couldn't afford to be affectionate nor emotional, except in extraordinary cases like the assassination of Martin Luther King, Jr. (all the adults cried then, Mama says)—or when they expressed anger at children who got out of line by whipping them. Back then, my family had to funnel the bulk of their energy toward surviving. They didn't have time to emote.

The largest slave auction in U.S. history took place in coastal Georgia, from where my maternal family hails, and is known as the "Weeping Time," even though, according to eyewitness accounts, few people sold over those two days wept. Under the pseudonym Q. K. Philander Doesticks, journalist Mortimer Thomson reported on the demeanors of people being sold at the auction for the *New York Tribune*:

"On the faces of all was an expression of heavy grief; some appeared to be resigned to the hard stroke of Fortune that had torn them from their homes, and were sadly trying to make the best of it; some sat brooding moodily over their sorrows, their chins resting on their hands, their eyes staring vacantly, and their bodies rocking to and fro, with a restless motion that was never stilled; few wept, the place was too public and the drivers too near, though some occasionally turned aside to give way to a few quiet tears."

✦

The buyers didn't even consider the Africans human, yet they chose to remain self-composed. The skies cried for them instead with buckets of pouring rain. When descendants of enslaved Africans cry, it is a powerful act. We cry because our ancestors couldn't.

Still, somehow my ancestors endured. Drawing from either resilience built on spiritual beliefs, devotion to one another, or both, they endured. I'm not sure how I would have gone on without the level of care I had at Duke because my resilience had run dry. I got connected to much-needed mental health care and haven't been in a psych ward since, for which I'm grateful. My hospital stay showed me the beauty in being vulnerable. My current therapist, who I've worked with for three years, is a Black queer counselor I connected with on the Therapy for Black Girls website. We met my second semester in graduate school when I felt myself descending into crisis and didn't know how much longer I could withstand racist microaggressions and leaving writing workshops feeling beat down. My first time on her office couch, I let my strong façade melt away instantly because I knew it was okay to cry. Now I know, crying releases endorphins and oxytocin that help alleviate our emotional, physical, and spiritual pain. It feels powerful to have another queer Black woman witness and affirm my tears.

The day I walked into Duke Hospital and the nurse asked me if I was always so teary, and I answered "no," she probably thought it was a good thing. Maybe I did, too. I've always admired the dignity of Black Americans who can hold back their tears in the face of adversity—but I've grown to see those who can't or won't as just as dignified. Despite all that our people have gone through, we're still here. Our capacity to cry means white enslavers failed to rob us of our ability to feel.

I cry to heal not only myself but also to heal my ancestors and descendants.

Nichol Young crabs in Brunswick, Georgia's Marshes of Glynn Overlook Park.

Water is Life

AFTER EIGHT YEARS OF PARTNERSHIP, IN FEBRUARY 2020, I finally showed my spouse, Jojo, the place I call home. My home lies in a southeastern pocket of Georgia by the Atlantic, Glynn County, home to Brunswick on the mainland (where I used to live) and St. Simons, Jekyll, and other small barrier islands. It's a five-hour drive from our home in the Atlanta area. We hadn't gone together yet because we had lived far away from Brunswick for most of our relationship. We got together in Atlanta in 2012, moved to Seattle for work two years later, then returned to Atlanta in 2018.

Returning to Georgia, I was apprehensive about visiting home. I had been away from Brunswick for nearly a decade and didn't feel like I would fit in there, having not lived there full-time since I was eighteen. I kept up with goings-on in my hometown through friends'

Facebook pages but since most of my family had moved away, I had no real reason to visit. Jojo asked to go there a few times, and I would always respond, "There's nothing for you there." I said this because I thought there was nothing there for *me*. I had been told since I was little to get out of there as fast as I could because it wasn't a place where Black people could thrive. Even when I started reporting on the area in 2018, I didn't feel like I necessarily belonged there.

An invitation to a February 2020 Gullah Geechee forum from the event's organizer, Aminata Traoré-Morris, brought me back home to Georgia's coast with my excited spouse in tow. It was held in Liberty County, too close to home to not visit. After the forum, I took Jojo to see the St. Simons Pier Village, a tourist's dream crowded with shops, restaurants, a park, a lighthouse, and a pier that juts out into the St. Simons Sound. I remembered how to get there without Google Maps. This was right before the pandemic began, so we inhaled the fishy sea air unobstructed. We smiled at a girl taking pictures in a pink quinceañera dress with young men wearing festive suits. We walked through Neptune Park, named after Neptune Small, an enslaved African who retrieved his master's corpse from the Civil War battlefield in Fredericksburg, Virginia, accompanying the casket all the way back to St. Simons. I pointed out indigenous live oak trees, sprawling beauties dripping with Spanish moss, regaling Jojo with the story of how I almost got my first kiss in one of them. After being away for so many years, it felt comforting to be home. The calm breeze, squawking gulls, squishy sand, and fish smell. Felt like I was surrounded by old friends. I thought about how lucky I was to have grown up in such a scenic place.

We walked down a set of stairs to the sliver of sand and shoreline on the other side of the "Johnson Rocks," a wall of large granite boulders built to prevent erosion, named after the president who initiated their construction, Lyndon B. Johnson. We snapped pictures of each other for the 'gram, then walked west toward the pier. As we walked, I saw a giant ship turned on its side in the water less than a mile away from the pier.

"That's the Golden Ray," I told my spouse. I'd heard on the news that in the wee hours of September 8, 2019, the 656-foot-long Hyundai cargo ship capsized in the St. Simons Sound with 4200 cars, twenty four crewmen, and 400,000 gallons of oil onboard as it departed from the Port of Brunswick. All the crewmen were saved, but nearly two years later, the Golden Ray still sat in the sound, slowly being dismantled section by section under the direction of a Unified Command consisting of the U.S. Coast Guard, the Georgia Environmental Protection Division, and Gallagher Marine Systems. The Unified Command was responsible for ensuring the wreckage removal abided by environmental protection standards set by the federal Oil Pollution Act of 1990.

The Golden Ray joined a long list of environmental issues in Glynn. Brunswick houses a cluster of factories with emissions visible in the air: thick white clouds that smell like rotting eggs. Thus, I always figured we had an air pollution problem. But I never considered the possibility of toxins in our water until researching the first story I wrote about my hometown's environmental history for *Autostraddle*, a site for LGBTQIA+ women and non-binary people. I interviewed the founder of Glynn Environmental Coalition (GEC), Daniel Parshley, who told me about his nonprofit's Safe Seafood Program, which aims to educate fishers in Glynn through direct outreach on how to reduce health risks when eating potentially contaminated local seafood.

Living by the ocean had always been one of the coolest parts of growing up on Georgia's coast. Eating from those beloved waters had felt like a treat. Hearing that I and people who I loved had likely eaten contaminated food back home disturbed me. I didn't like that it took me almost thirty years to find out this information. There isn't much reporting or research on the topic. Eating seafood is a way of life for Black people in coastal Georgia, who make up a majority of the region. It doesn't surprise me that this issue hasn't gotten much attention. I historically, the media and academia have ignored the problems of Black people in the Deep South. I feel like I would be letting my ancestors down if I didn't report on the toxins in our waters.

In my travels down this road, I've learned more about who I am and where I come from. I've realized that my family stuffing ourselves silly with a delectable blend of freshly caught crab and shrimp, sausage, corn on the cob, and potatoes with newspaper covering the table is part of a larger culture. Our relationship with water is different from that of Black people raised inland. The more I learned about the Gullah Geechee culture from various sources, including Julie Dash's 1991 film *Daughters of the Dust* and the Gullah Geechee forum that I attended, the more I suspected it applied to my maternal family, who've been rooted on the Georgia coast in Chatham, Liberty, and McIntosh counties for as long as we can remember. Coastal Georgia—along with the coastal areas of North Carolina, South Carolina, and Florida—is the home of Gullah Geechee peoples who've retained particular West African traditions in insulated communities, hybridizing them with American culture out of necessity. Some distinguish between the Gullah and the Geechee, stating the Gullah live in the Carolinas and the Geechee reside in Georgia and Florida. I'm aligned with those who see the two terms as interchangeable. The Gullah Geechee have their own distinct arts, crafts, foodways, and language.

"Gullah Geechee people have had an integral relationship and connection with the ocean for centuries, whether for their own livelihood and sustenance, for transportation, for supplementing their rations issued by plantation masters," the environmentalist and public historian Hermina Glass-Hill told me during my reporting. "It is a spiritual connection to the water as well, and of course, there's this historical remembrance of consciousness of the Middle Passage that they're deeply connected to."

In an interview from the African American Fishermen Oral History Project, Gullah Geechee historian Griffin Lotson explained that, in the past, being Geechee wasn't "cool" or a "good way to get ahead in society." This may explain why my family disassociated themselves from this identity. We may not call ourselves Geechee, but now that I better understand the term, I see my family in it. I understand the culture to be the self-sufficient, spiritual way of life developed by descendants of enslaved West Africans on the southeastern coast of the U.S.

Most of my relatives who fished to help sustain themselves, a Gullah Geechee tradition, have passed. Fortunately, my mother is still with us, and she shares bits of our Geechee heritage, even if she doesn't identify them as such. She recalls my grandmother's special nuggets of wisdom, such as to only eat oysters in months with names that include the letter "r," and how neighbors regularly supplied her family with seafood for free that they caught on the job. She told me that my own family worked in the seafood industry in McIntosh County, where they got work at the Meridian dock "heading" (removing the head from) shrimp and also at a seafood processing plant. Mama laments that her grandmother wouldn't allow her to head shrimps with her brother and mother.

Exactly a year after first seeing the Golden Ray's wreckage with my spouse, I returned to Glynn to explore how water pollution affects African-American and Gullah Geechee fishing culture in the county. The trip was part of my ongoing quest to reclaim a culture that society has attempted to erase. My itinerary over that Valentine's Day weekend: shadowing safe seafood outreach to subsistence fishers with Aaron Bell from GEC and collaborating with photographer Keamber Pearson. In addition to learning about and witnessing the polluted waterways, I also hoped to visit Igbo (or Ebo) Landing, a site on St. Simons's Dunbar Creek, where more than a dozen Igbo peoples from what is now Nigeria drowned themselves rather than be enslaved in May 1803.

It wasn't until college that I'd come across the story of the "Flying Africans," the mythologized version of the story, while writing a paper about Black history in Georgia for an African American studies course. According to an oral history collected in the 1930s from an old Black man named Wallace Quarterman by the Federal Writers' Project, after being brutally whipped by an overseer, a group of enslaved Africans "got together and stuck that hoe in the field and then…rose up in the sky and turned themselves into buzzards and flew right back to Africa."

My wife and I scouted out the location a few hours before Pearson's flight came in. It was a drizzly Friday evening. My GPS led us to a cul-de-sac, where we were met by a white girl of about ten sitting on a bike with a cat in her arms. My eyes darted from the girl and her cat to the palatial homes shaded by live oaks to a large rusty gate. Seeing no apparent sign of Igbo Landing, we drove away.

The next morning, I drove from my St. Simons hotel across the four-mile causeway to Sidney Lanier Bridge Park in Brunswick to meet Bell, GEC's Safe Seafood Outreach coordinator. The weather was gray but clear. I donned a Columbia jacket with a hood for the cold weather and possible rain, waterproof Keds, and a KN95 coupled with a cloth mask.

Prior to my trip, Bell told me that African Americans comprise the majority of subsistence fishers in the area. Fishing for Food, a research institute at Duke University, broadly defines a subsistence fisher as someone who depends on fish for survival; is low-income; lives close to the body of water where they fish; harvests fish to eat or sell to meet basic food requirements; uses low-technology gear as part of cultural practice; and/or relies on their harvest to meet their nutritional needs.

I could see there wasn't much activity in the park aside from a few people launching their boats into the Brunswick River. The river is part of the Turtle-Brunswick River estuary, home to the LCP Chemicals Superfund site, which consists of eight hundred thirteen acres of soil, groundwater, surface waters, and marshes that were contaminated by four different industries between the 1920s and 1994. Brunswick boasts a total of four Superfund sites, which have been designated for cleanup by the Environmental Protection Agency as the most hazardous sites in the country, and fourteen sites listed on Georgia's Hazardous Site Inventory. All but one of the hazardous sites in the small city, which is 55.1 percent Black, lies within a one-mile radius of a "majority-minority" population. Alternatively, predominantly white St. Simons has zero Superfund sites.

Among other substances, the LCP Chemicals site contains mercury and polychlorinated biphenyls (PCBs), which primarily affect people of childbearing age, children, and fetuses. They may cause lower IQs, a weakened immune system, and behavioral and psychological effects in children, and may cause thinning of the uterus lining, possibly leading to the need for its removal. Upon studying the rates of hysterectomies in Brunswick, GEC's founder discovered that he could correlate the rate of hysterectomies in the city to a population that has been heavily exposed to PCBs. In 2012, he assisted the

Agency for Toxic Substances and Disease Registry (ATSDR) with testing the blood of nine residents in Sapelo Island, twenty-five miles away from LCP Chemicals, who eat at least two meals of seafood a day. The study measured higher-than-normal levels of PCBs in their blood. These findings cause me to wonder whether these toxins had any bearing on excruciatingly painful periods that took me years to alleviate with an IUD and natural remedies.

A white man who graduated from my rival high school, Glynn Academy, a few years before I graduated from Brunswick High in the mid-2000s, Bell admits that some fishers may be loath to speak with him because he "looks like a cop." He showed me the handouts he distributes to fishers, a general brochure about fish you can catch and eat in Glynn County, another for people who are pregnant, planning to be pregnant, or nursing a child. The handouts display information on how to minimize risk by limiting consumption of certain seafood and using particular cleaning and cooking methods. The organization's work also includes providing technical assistance at Superfund sites, air and water quality monitoring, lobbying, community organizing, and education.

After about thirty minutes of waiting for fishers, we decided to move to another location. Bell said there would've been more fishers out if the weather were better. I followed Bell to Marshes of Glynn Overlook Park on the south end of Brunswick, where my tenth-grade boyfriend once took me crabbing. The park is a front-row seat to the "league and a league of marsh-grass, waist-high, broad in the blade" made famous by Confederate army veteran and poet Sidney Lanier (the bridge's namesake). It sits alongside the Mackay River, which is connected to Terry and Dupree creeks, home to the Terry Creek Superfund site where a manufacturer called Hercules specializing in extracting resins from pine stumps dumped toxaphene waste from 1948 to 1980. Banned in 1990, toxaphene was once a popular pesticide. The ATSDR reports convulsions and damage to the kidneys and liver in humans who have had significant exposure to toxaphene.

At Overlook Park, we spotted a Black man and woman fishing together. They sat in a red SUV to keep warm, getting out to check their net on the dock every so often. Bell and I approached their car and found out they were from Kingsland, about forty miles south of Brunswick. They were crabbing that day, had never heard about the seafood advisory, and wanted to know more. They asked about who conducted the research (GEC, the Glynn County Health Department, the Georgia Department of Public Health, the Georgia Department of Natural Resources, Sea Grant, and the University of Georgia) and where to find a safer place to crab. Bell suggested spots along the causeway to St. Simons with more inflow and outflow of fresh, clean water.

He also directed the pair's attention to billowing clouds of white smoke spouting out of a factory about a mile away as the culprit for the toxins. The factory is now known as Pinova; the site was purchased from the Hercules plant's parent company in 2010 and has changed hands a couple of times since. While Pinova rebranded itself as "sustainable" and doesn't dump hazardous waste, the company is still deemed a co-owner of a hazardous waste facility by the Georgia Environmental Protection Division (EPD). Pinova received Air Quality Act violations in 2016 and 2018 and is currently being investigated by the Georgia EPD and GEC for possibly contributing to a rotting garbage odor that frequently pervades downtown Brunswick. Bell never told the couple not to eat the crab they caught in the advisory area that day. His organization believes that an advisory isn't going to stop people from fishing in a particular body of water, especially those who fish as a cultural practice. Glynn's local waterways are as important of a resource as ever—since the pandemic started, GEC has observed an increase in local fishing activity.

Earlier, during a Zoom interview, GEC's executive director, Rachael Thompson, told me that some people become alarmed when they learn the nonprofit doesn't tell people not to eat the seafood in advisory areas, except for when an area is actually in and not just adjacent to a Superfund site. A young white woman wearing her brown hair on top of her head, dangly earrings, and large glasses, Thompson told me, "We teach people how to mitigate their risk. Our job is not to tell people what to do. Our job is to provide information for people to make decisions about their health." Her voice conveyed an earnest authority. "We're not a doctor. We're not PhD scientists over here. We have information that we think will help people make choices.... We don't want people to have these health impacts, but we also understand that for these subsistence fishermen and their families, this might be one of their very limited food sources. We don't want to exacerbate the food insecurity that already exists in this town."

At a fishing spot on Dupree Creek later that afternoon, Bell and I met two other crab fishers, one of them a Black male elder with a gray beard named Jimmy. He wore a dark work jumpsuit layered over a hoodie on his small frame and a baseball cap. His wife sat waiting in their car. Despite Jimmy's bucket full of blue crab, he told us he catches and cooks them for his wife and children, not himself. The other fisher, an amiable, stocky middle-aged white man, wasn't faring as well as Jimmy and asked for his technique. He told us he was a member of the Coast Guard, originally from Seattle, and living temporarily in St. Simons to help remove the Golden Ray.

After visiting a few more fishing spots along the causeway, I followed Bell's truck to the St. Simons Pier, where we examined the 71,000-ton ship and the VB-10,000, a giant yellow heavy-lift barge tasked with cutting and then transporting ship debris to a recycling facility. I couldn't help but feel tiny in comparison to this disaster scene. I watched two bottlenose dolphins swimming in unison, unfazed by the wreckage removal. Adults and children on the pier pointed at the animals and shouted with glee. I convinced myself that the two dolphins were a mother and child pair, two beings remaining resilient in the face of environmental degradation—a reflection of Black coastal Georgians.

Fletcher Sams, executive director of the Altamaha Riverkeeper, told me in a post-trip interview that the Golden Ray wreckage removal is shaping up to be one of the most expensive in U.S. history. His nonprofit monitors the vessel's environmental impacts. Sams said, "Since the morning of day one, we have been documenting damage done to the sound and the estuary. That could be anything, from collecting samples to mapping to documenting the location and times of shoreline impact to helping the Unified Command improve their mitigation strategy." There have been several releases of heavy fuel oil, a substance capable of causing cancer in living tissue, from the Golden Ray during the removal process, posing harm to both animals and humans who eat seafood caught in the sound. Sams told me he's disappointed the state has yet to conduct a Natural Resource Damage Assessment to quantify the ecological and economic harm caused by the shipwreck and formulate recommendations in an effort to reverse damages.

After leaving Bell and the mama and baby dolphin at the pier, the photographer, Pearson, and I met up with my spouse, and the three of us went looking again for Igbo Landing. The night before, a Twitter friend advised that they'd been able to see the approximate location of Igbo Landing from the Dunbar Creek Bridge. We parked at one end of the bridge and walked onto it to get a good view of the creek as cars whizzed by. I wondered what passersby were thinking as we, three Black queer people, walked on the bridge with such purpose in our steps and if they even knew the significance of Dunbar Creek.

We stood on a thin steel railing right on top of the winding creek. My spouse and I clasped hands, spoke to our ancestors, then dropped an offering of an orange into the water below. I envisioned it hitting the bottom of the creek, where the Igbo rebels' bodies once lay. Later that day, I found out the sacred creek is now full of sewage from a wastewater treatment plant, an indication of the destruction of coastal Georgia waters that sustain the bodies and spirits of Black people.

Water pollution is an affront to the Gullah Geechee way of life. Despite myriad structural obstacles, African Americans on St. Simons are fighting to preserve their ancestors' ways of life and connectedness to land and water. In the early 2000s, the St. Simons African American Heritage Coalition, a group of Black residents on the island, and the St. Simons Land Trust saved the Historic Harrington School from demolition by speculative developers. The building housed a grade school for Black children from the 1920s until they began getting bussed to the mainland in the 1950s and then a daycare center until 1970. The Library of Congress contains folk songs by the Georgia Sea Island Singers recorded at the schoolhouse in 1959 by the complicated ethnomusicologist Alan Lomax. A whitewashed clapboard building with a brick foundation and chimney, a deep roof overhang, and an adorable replica of the school out front doubling as a Little Free Library, the schoolhouse is a picturesque portal to the Harrington community's Gullah Geechee past. African Americans once owned eighty-six percent and populated seventy-five percent of the island but have been plagued with what journalist Patrik Jonsson calls a "tropical form of gentrification": The 2020 U.S. Census reported the island's Black population as two percent, and the median cost of homes sold on the island today is $665,000.

Driving through the neighborhood, you would never know the private event venue at Village Creek owned by a white family was once the location of a fish camp operated by legendary Geechee fisherman Cusie Sullivan until the 1960s. Born in 1896, he worked as a fishing guide, and rented and sold equipment and refreshments to local fishermen. Author Jingle Davis writes of Sullivan in her book, *Island Time*, "He knew where and when the fish were biting, what bait to use, how deep to fish, and whether high or low ebb would yield a mess of speckled trout or spottail bass."

Helen Ladson, former tour guide at the Historic Harrington School, told me about what Sullivan meant to his community via email: "Fishing was a source of life in many ways on the coast. On St. Simons Island, Mr. Cusie Sullivan owned one of the most popular fishing camps, now known as Village Creek. This fishing camp served as a source of income to sustain life on the island for the Harrington community. Mr. Sullivan and crew would take visitors out on the marsh to the best fishing sites. Fishing was also a source of protein that was served during mealtime. Fish was prepared in multiple ways: smoked, fried, grilled, baked, or blackened. Fish and grits, shrimp and grits, & crab boil were other delicacies that were and still are consumed."

The environmentalist and historian, Glass-Hill, pointed out to me how African Americans have been edged out of coastal Georgia's commercial fishing industry. "They were fishermen and oyster men and did all kinds of jobs on the ocean. That kind of livelihood has become so commercialized. It's really hard to compete and get a profit when you're competing against such large commercial fishing indus-tries," she said. Dr. Dionne Hoskins-Brown, founder of the African American Fishermen Oral History Project, attributes the decline of Black fishermen in coastal Georgia to increased fishing costs, little access to capital, and parents discouraging their children from work-ing in labor-intensive fisheries professions.

I have faith that Gullah Geechee fishing culture isn't going any-where as long as Gullah Geechee peoples live, breathe, and eat. A month after my recent trip to Glynn, I met Queen Quet, Chieftess of the Gullah/Geechee Nation, at the virtual Coastal Cultures Conference (it's usually held on St. Helena Island, South Carolina, Queen Quet's home). Eleven years ago, Queen Quet helped found the Gullah/Geechee Fishing Association, which advocates for the indigenous fishing rights of Gullah Geechee and African-American fishers and fishery workers in the southeast. They organize against environmental threats to Gullah Geechee fishing culture, such as flooding and offshore drilling. At the conference, we watched a clip from *Gwine Fishin'*, a documentary compiled by the Nation over twenty years that tells the plight of Gullah Geechee fishers in South Carolina, who are targeted by the Department of Natural Resources with exorbitant fines for simply "fishing while Black." The association is fighting for a subsistence fishing bill in South Carolina.

I'd read about Queen Quet in the media for years, so I felt excited and nervous in her virtual presence. A Black woman whose looks are indeed regal, she presided over the conference with shells in her twisted hair. She switched effortlessly between using the Gullah language and the Queen's English, drawing from ancestral and spir-itual knowledge, and her mathematics and computer science back-ground, too. She made sure we knew that we were in a sacred space. Her disappointment with the media's typical portrayal of her culture stuck with me. She mentioned recent coverage by journalist Soledad O'Brien and model and food show host Padma Lakshmi that focused on the disappearance of Gullah Geechee culture instead of its preservation and the ways in which it is still flourishing. I resolved to highlight with my writing what's at stake of being lost if we continue to ignore the culture instead of what's already been lost. I want to keep the fire burning, not extinguish it.

Before the conference adjourned, each attendee shared a little about ourselves. After I spoke about how I haven't historically claimed Gullah Geechee despite my suspected Gullah Geechee heritage, Queen Quet said, "You may not claim us, but we're still going to claim you." A fellow attendee chimed in, saying she once stood in my shoes. "After you begin identifying as Gullah Geechee, the rest of your family will follow," she advised. Exiting out of Zoom, I felt like Sethe in *Beloved*, when Paul D tells her she is her best thing. I felt like I was enough. Queen Quet affirmed that it was okay to claim Gullah Geechee without my family's permission. So now I wonder if my Gullah Geechee ancestors wail each time their precious waters are desecrated.

*In June 2023, the resin manufacturing company Pinova released a statement announcing the permanent closure of their facility after more than one-hundred years of operating in the Brunswick community, citing "destroyed core production assets and infrastructure" that would require "substantial demolition, reconstruction, costs and time." Two months prior, a massive fire broke out at Pinova, ceasing operations and garnering criticism from Brunswick Mayor Cosby Johnson, who pledged to form a committee to further investigate the fire a few weeks before the announcement. After a century of polluting the area, the company is divesting in Brunswick-Glynn County. Pinova is still responsible for environmental cleanup at the site under the supervision of Georgia's Environmental Protection Division. At the time of publication, there are no concrete plans for the property once the plant closes.

Neesha at Etowah Indian Mounds in Bartow County, Georgia, the traditional territories of the Woodland Indians, Mississippian Mound Builders, and the Cherokee and Muscogee (Creek) nations.

September

YAHA

The tour guide calls our class's attention to an alligator on a log, napping to a symphony of songbirds and swaying bald cypress trees. Y2K is around the corner, and we're on a field trip at the Okefenokee Swamp. Our lives are in the hands of a tour guide captain, a middle-aged white man whose name I can't remember. Since we are under twelve and got a children's discount, the tour cost us each less than twenty bucks. During the one-hour bus ride to our destination, kids joked about who would get eaten first.

Mr. Tour Guide is expected to save two dozen of us from the whims of a thirty-five-mile-per-hour-running reptile with an appetite for small mammals. He is the only protector on our long white canoe in the middle of miles of black water. This 400,000-acre wetland, the traditional territories of the Timucua peoples near the Georgia-Florida border, is now his domain. White men claimed it as theirs hundreds of years ago, falsely believing land is intended to be owned as products of a feudal society. I am supposed to trust this man, but I don't. He is a stranger with the same skin color as the kids who call me "nigger." I can't stop my foot from shaking. There are an estimated ten thousand alligators in the surrounding water, no known attacks, but I'm not privy to this knowledge. So I wonder if the reptiles are hungry for human flesh, hungry to conquer like those white colonizers.

Thirty years from now, a white-owned company will apply for a permit to open a mine by this swamp, threatening all the wildlife we're here to see—and burial grounds of the Muscogee (Creek) Nation.

YUCHA

If you're curious about the Timucua, you won't find anything about them on the Okefenokee Swamp's website. You won't find out what Okefenokee means either. It could derive from a Muscogee word for bubbling water, oki fanôki. Or, from a Creek word meaning "trembling land." Timucua may originate from a term one of their enemy tribes used to refer to them, Thimogoua, or the Spanish mispronunciation of atimoqua, the Timucuan word for "lord" or "chief." Before their extinction, the Timucua had thirty-five chiefdoms in southeast Georgia and North Florida. The last Timucuans are said to have either left for Cuba on a boat in 1763 or been taken in by other Indigenous groups.

Our tour guide didn't share this information with us. Perhaps he thought it insignificant. I hope he didn't withhold it intentionally. Native American history was rarely taught at my elementary school until Thanksgiving came around. I once graced my local newspaper in kindergarten wearing a pilgrim costume. Reading my picture book of Christopher Columbus "discovering" the Americas, I made no value judgments; although, I visually identified with the colorful, feathered brown-skinned people with jet black hair. The only Native Americans I knew at the time lived inside an electronic tube. From bed, Mama watched black and white "cowboys and Indians" movies on weekends. I saw Native American cartoon characters (usually voiced by non-Natives) far more than actual Native American actors. I didn't know any Indigenous folks in real life, as far as I knew.

On the morning of my eighth birthday, Mama gave me my gifts by spreading them out on her bed: a smorgasbord of Pocahontas, the first Disney princess to look remotely like me with her sepia-colored skin. I loved everything about the rebellious character and found her attractive. Among the presents was a soundtrack CD with a book of lyrics, which included a song loosely based on an Algonquin language that implores the Great Spirit to help Pocahontas's people "keep the ancient ways." I boisterously sang the chant at the beginning and end of the song, pretending to dance by the sacred fire: "Hega hega yah-pi-ye-hega/Yah-pi-ye-he-he hega." It felt like the cousin of the clapping, dancing, jumping, and shouting that shook my Black Missionary Baptist church each Sunday. It felt joyful.

HAPU

"Woahhh ohhh ohhh ohhh," my cheer squad warbles to the tune of the band playing in front of us, our right hands making a chopping gesture. We're cheering on our middle school football team, the red and black Needwood Warriors. I'm standing beside a friend who I consensually touch on during practice. We touch each other, not sexually but playfully. It gives me a rush. I'm crushing on her; although,

I would never admit it because no one is openly gay at my school. I only see gay people on TV.

A white male teacher with a brown ponytail wearing Native American garb stands in the distance, and nobody questions whether it's cultural appreciation or appropriation. Native American costumery is ubiquitous here, and we are all blissfully ignorant or at least we behave that way. A group of parents and students voted for the Warrior to be our mascot to channel the spirit and strength of "Georgia's first Americans." The Warrior's side profile graces a wall of our cafeteria: a chisel-faced man with red warpaint across his nose and a red and white headdress.

I cringe when I see myself tomahawk chopping on the morning announcements, a goofy grin spread across my face. I wish I could hide inside of my shirt. We all look terribly silly. None of us are Native American; I know of only one Native American kid in the entire school. Nevertheless, I dutifully chop whenever I hear those familiar notes. We chop and chop and chop away, never knowing we're cheering on Timucua land.

CHEQUETA

I stretch my legs out, resting them on the back of the seat in front of me. It's the mid-2000s, and I'm sitting in a college lecture hall with my friend, Alexa, waiting for class to start.

Alexa examines my legs.

"Your skin is red like an Indian's...you got Indian in your family, girl?" she asks.

"Who knows?" I reply.

I am tickled by the question, a little flattered even. I've been asked if I was mixed with white before, but this feels a whole lot cooler.

＊

Almost every African American at some point wonders whether our great-grandmother with high cheekbones and straight black hair hanging down to her butt or whether our own loose curls mean we got "Indian" in our family. I think it makes us feel better, like at least not *all* our ancestors came over in chains. Being Black and Native American is seen as infinitely more special and exotic than being plain old Black. Black American guests on Henry Louis Gates Jr.'s PBS genealogy show, *Finding Your Roots*, are always surprised when family rumors of Native American ancestry are proven wrong via DNA. Gates tells them Black people with Native American heritage are a lot less common than we think.

Still, the myth of the Black and Native great-grandmother persists. When another Black girl at school had long, straight hair without putting a chemical relaxer in it, I thought to myself with a tinge of envy, "She must got Indian in her family." She had won the genetic lottery because she didn't have to waste hours with smelly paste burning her scalp like most of us fully Black girls.

MARUA

I am on the phone in my rundown office on the southside of Seattle in 2014, chatting with an elderly white activist. We've met once or twice at meetings. Our conversation about organizing public housing tenants drifts to other topics, like the Duwamish tribe, whose land Seattle occupies, and their fight for federal recognition.

"By the looks of it, you've got Native American blood in you," the lady says.

I tell her she is mistaken. I have my suspicions, but I don't want to be misconstrued as claiming an Indigenous identity. I am more aware of whose land I'm on than ever living in a state with twenty-nine Indian reservations, a stark contrast to my home state Georgia's zero. It's easy for people in Georgia to talk about Indigenous peoples as if they're all gone. Not here though. Here, I attend events where land acknowledgements are spoken first, brief statements made in respect to the Native American tribes whose land we inhabit. The city is named after a Duwamish and Suquamish chief who befriended white settlers, who in turn expelled Chief Seattle's people from their ancestral home. I wouldn't dare say, "I might have Indian in my family," in this achingly beautiful environment. I literally cried as Jojo and I drove on the edge of Washington state's snow peaked mountains dotted with evergreens on our trek from down south. The Duwamish are the rightful keepers of these lush, enchanting lands. It infuriates me to think about their tribe being denied their right to self-governance and federal funding for decades.

One of my first Thanksgivings in Seattle, Jojo and I eat dinner with two friends, another couple. One of them is an enrolled member of a Coast Salish tribe, but we don't discuss the irony of him being here. He's here to spend time with friends, not to celebrate. Somehow, we end up watching *Pocahontas* on VHS after dinner, and when I hear the familiar Algonquin chant of my childhood, I instinctually belt it out. A sharp look from my wife stops me mid-chant, and my face burns. Our Coast Salish friend doesn't say a word, but I am still ashamed. I'm not an eight-year-old nor a middle schooler anymore. I now know Pocahontas's story is about colonization, genocide, and trafficking, not a romance between her and the Englishman John Smith like Disney portrays. I know you shouldn't wear traditional Indigenous clothes as a costume. I know Indigenous songs aren't meant for me to sing—they're for the descendants of those who fought and died to preserve them. I know they are sacred. I know you shouldn't adopt another culture's customs without their explicit permission, and even then, you walk a fine line between appreciation and appropriation. I ask myself, am I no better than the "white man"?

I silently vow to do better. I act unbothered as we watch the rest of the movie, even jeering at John Smith, but I'm secretly disturbed by my own ignorance.

MARECA

Sitting in my office chair at the tenants' union, I spit into a tube with vigor. This tube and this spit hold the key to reconstructing lineage lost in the Middle Passage. This is redemption for the times in school when I couldn't answer, "Where is your family from?" As a Christmas gift to myself, I forked over $99 to 23andMe for an ancestry DNA test.

My mother gets excited when I tell her about the test. "You know we have Indian in our family, right? My grandmother who you never met, my dad's mom, used to tell me her grandmother, September, was an Indian with long hair down her back who lived in South Carolina." Mama never mentioned this before, but I'm not surprised. Every Black American family has a September.

A month goes by. I hungrily scan my DNA test results as soon as they hit my inbox: 75.6 percent West African, 9.4 percent Congolese and Southern East African, 12.1 percent European, one percent Chinese and Southeast Asian…and 0.4 percent Native American. This means 0.4 percent of my DNA matches Native American samples in 23andMe's database. Being this percentage Native American means my most recent fully Native American ancestors roamed the earth two hundred to three hundred years ago. September was probably more white than Native American.

When Mama hears the news, she sounds disappointed. We got "Indian" in our family—but it's extremely distant. Just enough for the Americas on my 23AndMe ancestry composition map to be colored in yellow. Across the Atlantic, Africa is colored in purple. My DNA comprises 31.5 percent Nigerian, 29.9 percent Ghanaian, Liberian, and Sierra Leonean, and 8.6 percent Angolan and Congolese, among myriad other African ethnicities. I felt a smidge of disappointment about lacking Native American ancestry because I grew up believing it would make me important and special. I'd internalized anti-Black beliefs in our culture that say being just plain Black isn't good enough. But I quickly shifted my focus to the pride I felt in being majority African. I like thinking about how my ancestors have found intimacy and companionship in their own communities for thousands of years, even after being stolen and displaced to another continent. I've had conversations with my Rwandan spouse where they say, "African people are always left out of conversations about indigeneity in the United States, but we are Indigenous, too. We are indigenous to our different regions of Africa." I may be an Indigenous African, but still, I have no claim to the native dances, songs, food, and customs of my ancestors. I am indefinitely unmoored. When I wear the mushanana of my wife's culture for special occasions, a sash draped over one shoulder and a wraparound skirt, I'm not sure if it's an act of appreciation or appropriation. But I am sure it makes me feel beautiful and makes my wife happy.

PIQICHA

It's a drizzly day in Atlanta, where we have moved back to from Seattle. Jojo and I are both on holiday break and want to do something outside our norm. We decide to visit the Etowah Indian Mounds less than an hour away. Etowah is a Muscogee word for town or trail crossing. It is afternoon when we walk into the building at the historic site, where we are the only visitors. We pay our six dollars each and go on our own private tour of the museum. We read the stories of the prehistoric ancestors to the Muscogee Creek, the Indigenous peoples of the South Appalachian Mississippian culture, who are responsible for building the site's six earthen mounds between 1000 and 1550 A.D. A thousands-years-old culture and society vanquished by Europeans' smallpox, measles, and violence.

After circling the entire museum, we step outside to face the towering mounds. Ten-foot-high Mound C is the only one that's been completely excavated, offering clues on a way of life full of arts, games, worship, and ceremonies. The tallest of them, The Temple Mound or Mound A, stands sixty-three-feet high, equivalent to a six-story building. It was likely a platform for the home of the chief. We walk up the stairs of the Temple Mound, taking care not to slip on the slick steps. Pleased with our mini workout, we snap a selfie at the top. We take another with the Etowah River in the background. Unlike in Okefenokee all those years ago, I am my own tour guide now. I choose which displays to engage with and read them critically since they were likely written by employees of our racist state government. I interpret what I'm seeing for myself. I'm no longer reliant upon a white man.

We are browsing the gift shop about to leave when two Black men with locs walk in the door and buy tickets. I wonder why they've shown up less than an hour before the site closes. Jojo and I give them a nod of solidarity as fellow Black people appreciating Indigenous culture. Maybe they, too, recognized the links between people indigenous to the Americas and indigenous Africans—how both groups lived in harmony with nature before being colonized and are currently reclaiming ancestral land and cultural traditions. The more we learn about each other, the more empathy we can foster for our different but similar struggles.

Back in our car, we start planning trips to other nearby Indian mounds.

PIQINAHU

I come across an article about gender-variant and queer Timucuans on Twitter. I already know Indigenous tribes have included gender-expansive people and same-gender relationships since their inception but never thought about them living on the land of my hometown. I can't find much on the topic, but an academic article by Heather Martel in the *Journal of the History of Sexuality* enumerates the differences between how the French and the Spanish interacted with the Timucuans when they arrived on their land in the 1500s. Spaniards perpetrated physical and sexual violence onto them, while the Huguenots, French Protestants, enacted a policy of "allurement" with the tribe, performing love and friendship. As the Huguenots cultivated this amiable relationship, they also wrote lies to people back home about the Timucuans being perverse while also rejecting "hermaphrodites" and "sodomites" in their society. To them, a culture accepting of queerness was inherently savage and depraved.

I wish I could've learned about gender-expansive and sexually diverse Timucuans growing up, how their culture viewed loving the same gender as natural and normal, how I was far from the first queer person on Georgia's coast. I wish their legacy wasn't strategically left out of history books. Since I rarely saw myself in history lessons, learning about Timucuans who diverged from sexuality and gender norms would have been affirming. Maybe I wouldn't have repressed my queerness until college if I'd known queer people have *always* been here. It would have shown me Indigenous peoples aren't as "other" as my teachers made them out to be.

I resonate with Indigenous cultures that acknowledge more than two genders exist, that a person can embody more than one gender, and that intimate relationships between any gender are valid. How I love and who I am will never be fixed. My identity can change with the weather, the season, the location of the planets, the alignment of the stars. But the western world is too rigid to accept this way of being. We're forced to label ourselves and to then stick to those labels. We're taught particular identities are attached to shame. The Timucua knew of no such thing. We have a lot to learn from Indigenous peoples throughout the world about how to live without shame. Colonialism teaches us to do the opposite quite literally by dictating school curriculum and controlling our culture, our media narratives, the very stories we internalize.

Sometimes I feel like I'm drowning in this country's puritanism. I wish I could be free. But is freedom attainable in a place founded on bloodshed and plundering?

Note: Each section header is a number from the extinct Timucua language. They are in chronological order from one to eight. I use them here in an effort to resist the erasure of my hometown's Indigenous peoples. I consider this an act of cultural exchange.

Polaroid photo of siblings Neesha, Mike, and Nicole, taken by Dad during the summer of 1994.

A Rolling Stone / Papa Was

I MET MY FATHER WHEN I WAS SIX.

It's possible I met him before then but was too young to remember. He may have been present at the family reunion where I was awarded a certificate for being the youngest family member. I was an infant at the time, so I don't remember. I know he drove down to Brunswick, Georgia, when I was born to buy my mother a station wagon, which she drove so long that rusted out holes formed in its ceiling. Those holes were a perfect representation of the fraught communication between Mama and my father, but I didn't know that back then. No one ever told me if he came to meet me when I was a newborn. I know he wasn't there for my birth. All I knew was my parents met and married in the Bronx, had my sister Nicole and me three years later, divorced shortly after my birth, and settled back in their rural Southern hometowns: hers in coastal Georgia and his in eastern North Carolina.

I knew my dad only through photos of him posing in front of his trailer. He was tall with light brown skin and glasses, like me, and wore fancy suits with a medallion around his neck. Everything else about him was a mystery.

✦

After completing his studies each day, a Dutch man in one of his rooms at an Italian university writes by candlelight. It casts a warm glow on his sleepy eyes and hollowed cheeks. Named Erasmus, he sips wine to alleviate the pain of his gallstones. His quill moves over papyrus as he recalls proverbs he's encountered over his forty-something years. Erasmus pens two versions of the same phrase: "A rolling stone does not gather algae" in Greek, and in Latin, "A rolling stone is not covered with moss."

After being canonized and serving briefly as a priest, Erasmus studied and taught at the University of Paris, Cambridge, Oxford, the University of Turin, and the Old University of Leuven; although, he preferred life as an independent scholar. He fell in love with a fellow canon, a man, to whom he wrote love letters. He enjoyed taking trips with beautiful young men.

Erasmus was the original rolling stone.

✦

When I was six and Nicole was nine, Mama dropped us off at Embassy Suites where our dad was staying. I felt like my comfort blanket had been whisked away. Mama wasn't there to speak for me or make sure I said the right things, which made my stomach churn with anxiety and excitement. In the hotel lobby, I shyly embraced my dad, who felt like a familiar stranger. He was wearing black from head to toe, a fedora, and a gold chain with the medallion I'd seen in photos. I wore a hat myself, a hot pink baseball cap turned slightly sideways, with matching overalls.

He didn't have memories of me like he did with my sister, who he nicknamed "Honeybee." I remember we ate Pizza Hut, but I don't remember what we said to each other. I thought he sounded like a smooth talker from New York City. After that meeting, Nicole and I started having long conversations with him on our kitchen phone. For my seventh birthday, he sent me a Super Nintendo with *Super Mario* and *Aladdin*, games I played religiously. At some point, I thought, this having a dad thing just might be okay.

A few months after our first meeting, my father picked me and Nicole up to spend the summer with him and Mike, the youngest of three half brothers whom we'd never met. I wasn't too nervous about the trip since Nicole would be by my side. I bubbled over with curiosity as I counted down the days before Dad came. I felt like Laura Ingalls Wilder of my beloved *Little House on the Prairie* books, a young girl on her way to discover the unknown. I would be fearless like her. I would conquer any obstacle. I would be a little pioneer, an adventurer. We got our hair braided before the trip because Mama knew Dad wouldn't know what to do with it. Mama bought us new clothes from a department store. She helped me stuff a big duffle bag with clothes, then I added a mountain of books. I felt like I was officially a big girl at seven years old.

At the crack of dawn, my father used his car phone to let us know he was down the street. When I got to the car, I spotted Mike inside.

We exchanged shy greetings. He looked like your average thirteen year old, wearing a baseball cap, an oversized T-shirt, and jean shorts. We were family but still strangers, so we didn't do much talking as we drove nearly seven hours north on I-95, the longest trip I'd ever taken. We drove past the South of the Border with its faux-Mexican tourist attractions between the two Carolinas, and I gazed wistfully out the window at its amusement park. It was the most exciting scenery of our trip. Hours passed with nothing but trees lining the highway.

The further we got away from home, the more independent I felt. My first time away from Mama. Dad was my guardian for the summer, but he didn't feel like a parent yet. As the blues blared from his car radio, I daydreamed about what would unfold over the next two months. Would I have fun? Would I become a daddy's girl? Would my paternal grandmother dote on me like my other one? Would Mike be overprotective like the big brothers on TV? Would I not want to leave by the end of the summer?

The trip ended in Kelford, North Carolina, a town of two hundred residents and one stoplight. It made the small city of Brunswick look metropolitan. On Baccarat Road, to this day, my father and his mother's trailers are the only homes for miles, surrounded by low, flat plains. The trailers sit perpendicular to each other. My grandmother's is dwarfed from behind by a big, old white clapboard building—a former segregated Black school my grandmother and her husband, Mr. Bobby, ran as a club when I was a kid. The club shared a name with the school once operated there, the Village Hideaway. In front of Grandma E's trailer stands a long power line; behind it are acres of pine trees. As we got out of the car, the midday sun bore down on our faces while bugs and birds chirped their welcomes. Dad showed me and Nicole the room where we would be sleeping on the far right end of the trailer. When I sat on the bed, it jiggled.

"Ever slept on a waterbed?" Dad asked.

I'd only seen waterbeds on TV. I launched myself onto the bed, and Nicole followed. It seesawed underneath us as we released our cooped up energy from the car ride.

It wasn't easy to reconcile my father's country surroundings with his sophisticated façade. Not only did he have a waterbed but also a jacuzzi. He played Bob Marley's "I Shot the Sheriff" loudly in the morning. One night, in the living room, he organized a talent show competition where he and I went up against Nicole and Mike. It was such a serious affair we broke out the typewriter to transcribe our songs. My dad taught us how to jab while regaling us with stories of boxing overseas in the army where they called him "Donnie Black," a play on his first name, Donnell. One of his fight posters occupied a place of pride on his living room wall: him and his opponent in fighting stance, ready to pummel each other's faces in. I detected pride in his voice when he reminisced about parachuting into enemy territory as part of the 82nd Airborne Division.

Sometimes, we would all lie on the waterbed and listen to relaxation tapes of a woman's soothing voice speaking self-affirmations. Each day was a new adventure. I didn't have time to miss Mama because I was busy taking in all the newness. Still, I couldn't imagine living there beyond the summer; it was too in the middle of nowhere. I never found out if Mike was overprotective because there was nothing and nobody out there to protect me from. We had to drive nearly an hour to get to major stores and restaurants. I wondered, how did such a traveled man with such worldly interests end up in a place like Kelford?

By the seventeenth century, one French-English dictionary defined a rodeur as "a vagabond, roamer, wanderer, street-walker, highway-beater; a rolling stone, one that does nought but runne here and there, trot up and downe, rogue all the country over." Being a rolling stone served Erasmus well as one of the bestselling authors of his time. A rolling stone came to be synonymous with a person who shirks their duties—but things are never that simple, are they?

*

At the time of my Kelford summer, my dad hadn't been a full-time father for years. He did the best he could to fulfill this role. I didn't know then that he was struggling with demons I was too young to understand. I mostly remember the fun times. "Driving" my father's car while sitting on his lap. Picking out my own clothes each day, something my mother didn't allow. Bathing as little as I wanted. Playing the girl characters on *Mortal Kombat*. Watching MTV and Nickelodeon late into the night. Listening to Mike's stories of growing up in NYC and singing with the Boys Choir of Harlem. Eating at fast food restaurants. Hanging out outside with Mookie the dog. Playing the *Pac-Man* arcade game and dancing on the stage at my grandmother's club.

But not everything was fun. Dad had satellite TV, and we kids planned our days around what we wanted to watch. When I saw one morning on the TV Guide channel that *Homeward Bound: An Incredible Journey* was coming on later that day, I just had to see it. What could be more epic than talking pets? I hunkered down on the living room couch in front of the TV hours before the movie started. Dad moseyed in at some point.

"Let me see the remote." Dad grabbed the remote and turned to TV Guide. "My fight's coming on at six. You kids are gonna have to find something else to do."

Hot tears crowded my eyes. "But *Homeward Bound* comes on then. It's a new movie I've been waiting to watch *all day*," I whined.

"Can't you watch it some other time? It's not that important."

"I wanna watch my movie," I shrieked, tears rolling down my face.

"Why do you have to be such a brat?" my father yelled.

He stomped to his bedroom and slammed the door. He didn't come back out for hours, so I got to watch my movie. The victory felt bittersweet. I got what I wanted but only at the expense of angering my dad for the first time. Despite our late start, I wished I could predict a happy ending for us, like in *Homeward Bound* when the old golden retriever Shadow finds his way home after injuring his leg and being left behind by his fellow travelers. But even at that tender age, I knew in the real world happy endings weren't promised.

My fantasy of having a perfect dad had been fractured. It became more fragile the night he burst into the front door and ran to his room. I was lying in my regular spot on the living room carpet between the TV and the coffee table, and Mike and Nicole sat on the couch as we watched music videos (I was especially intrigued by a new rapper named Da Brat who wore her hair in little girl twists and dressed like a boy). My siblings and I looked at each other with perplexed faces.

After a few minutes, Dad walked back out of his room with wind in his steps and a pistol in hand. He must've seen my eyes widen with fear. I'd never seen a gun in real life.

"Something's going down next door at the club. Y'all will be fine. Just stay inside and lock the door."

I felt scared but strangely excited. This would never happen at home. After Dad left, my siblings came up with different scenarios of why he needed his gun. My heart pumped faster the entire night, even though no shots were fired. Things went back to normal the next morning, and we kids never found out what transpired at the club.

But I remember how confused it left me. Dad exhibited aggression and exuded masculine energy to which I didn't know how to react. I didn't know how to exist around an angry man because I'd never had to. I couldn't predict Dad's actions like I could with Mama. The sheer possibility of somebody getting shot that night both frightened and intrigued me.

Those two months in 1994 were the first and last extended period of time Nicole and I spent with our dad. Afterwards, we continued talking to him over the phone every now and then. As we got older, Mama became more comfortable speaking negatively of him to us. One day when we aggravated her by lazing around instead of doing our chores, she started listing all the things she spent money on for us: food, clothes, cheerleading uniforms and camps, dance lessons. She said we were ungrateful.

"I do everything for y'all," Mama yelled. "The only thing Donnell's good for is the Social Security money y'all get from him every month. He doesn't even pay child support."

Our mother made it clear our father was a loser. I would be sitting at the dinner table, and she would shudder and say, "Stop making that face. You look just like Donnell." When I did something that reminded her of him, she would say she hoped I didn't turn out like him. She would mention my father "got sick" before I was born but was vague about his illness. She said he had something like a heart attack, but I could sense there was more to the story.

Dad visited me and Nicole in Brunswick less than a handful of times after our summer with him. I didn't think he was showing up enough to earn the title of "parent." It didn't feel like he was trying and because Mama spoke so poorly of him, I began emotionally distancing myself from my father. I grew resentful. I had so many questions. Where was he for the first five years of my life? Why wasn't he more present? Why did he make six children with four different women over a span of two decades? Calls between me and my father dwindled. Around middle school, during a rare conversation, he asked me why I didn't call him more often.

"*You're* the adult, not me, so *you're* responsible for us having a relationship," I retorted.

Dad didn't agree. I wouldn't speak to him again until about a decade later. He stopped calling both me and my sister. I suppose we were too proud to pick up the phone and call him. Mama and Nicole blamed me for my father not coming around anymore because of what I said. He called my maternal grandmother to ask if he could attend Nicole's high school graduation but failed to show up. He didn't even ask about mine when the time came, cementing his status in my head as a deadbeat. No one else noticed he didn't call, or if they did, they didn't mention it. But I noticed, and I washed my hands of him. He didn't deserve to see me graduate at the top of my class anyway. He hadn't been there to support me. I'm sure he had no idea when I graduated from college. I know I sure didn't tell him.

I've always associated the term "rolling stone" with men.

Somewhere along the line, the term became a euphemism for a man with questionable morals and behavior. There's that old song by The Temptations, "Papa Was a Rollin' Stone," about a rambling man who makes his home wherever he lies his hat. Then there's the legendary rock band, The Rolling Stones, British chaps known for partying wildly with groupies in their heyday. I think the rolling stone label fits my dad, who hopped from bed to bed, deposited his seed, and then moved on to a new pursuit.

We expect men to be rolling stones because they're seen as slaves to their hormones. They're not expected to be responsible for their "dirty deeds." But we rarely think of women as rolling stones. We think of women whose lives exist outside of mainstream acceptance as sluts, slobs, or junkies instead. A woman who bedhops, overindulges, or wanders aimlessly through the world isn't celebrated nor excused like a man who does the same. Women are expected to be accountable for our mistakes, to carry the world on our shoulders. We're not allowed to not have everything figured out. If our lives aren't completely "together," we're viewed as a failure. We're not allowed to be free.

I learned I couldn't get away with the same things boys could at fifteen after losing my so-called virginity to my boyfriend, Steven, a Chinese boy in the grade above me. I no longer believe in the concept of virginity, but I definitely did back then. I had planned to remain abstinent until marriage and even counseled middle and high school students over the phone for a small stipend at a local teen abstinence nonprofit. I encouraged my peers to stay true to their abstinence pledges. All that went out the window once I met Steven. Both "virgins," we were in love with the idea of love. He played Musiq Soulchild for me nonstop and even made a website dedicated to our love. I sang Kelly Clarkson's "A Moment Like This" to him in my driveway. We didn't have much in common besides being physically attracted to each other. But I was addicted to receiving romantic and sexual attention from him after years of being teased by boys. He picked me up for school every morning, and we hung out every afternoon.

A lot of our classmates were sexually active, so doing "it" didn't seem like a big deal. We snuck around and lied to our parents to find places to have sex. I insisted he wear a condom because I knew teenage motherhood wasn't for me, and eventually Mama took me to get birth control. She was disappointed in me. I only told my closest friends about my emerging sex life, while Steven bragged about it to whomever would listen. Between classes, we hung outside class-room doors until we couldn't any longer. Teachers often broke us up. A Black Caribbean male teacher scolded me as he walked past us standing outside my Algebra II class: "That's no way for a young lady to behave." As if Steven wasn't also culpable. At the homecoming dance, we danced no raunchier than anyone else. Yet a Black female teacher, the mother of a friend, pulled me to the side and hissed, "Cut. It. Out." I told her I hadn't done anything, but it didn't matter. I felt as if I were wearing a scarlet letter on my chest.

Those Black teachers probably meant well. They knew how society treats "fast" Black girls: like utter trash. Sexually active Black girls are accused of disrespecting their bodies, their elders, and their culture. White girls on my cheer squad weren't marked by their sexual activi-ties like I was. I suppose Black teachers wanted to "save" me before the real world chewed me up and spit me out. An early lesson in misogy-noir, the patriarchal, racist system that undermines the humanity and freedom of Black women, girls, and femmes. Black girls learn while we can't be a rolling stone, we must be hard as one. We're forced to shed our softness sooner than white girls. We're conditioned to be steady, a different kind of rock.

My white male principal tried to control my body, too. When Steven and I both signed up to go on a BETA Club trip to Atlanta, the principal pulled me to the side in the hallway beforehand, walkie talkie in hand: "Now look, I don't want any trouble out of you and Steven in Atlanta." I don't remember if or how I responded, but I remember feeling shocked. Did he think we were going to fuck on the bus? I felt as if he were my overseer.

We were nearing the end of fall semester when Steven clashed with his teammate, Carlton, in the football locker room. Carlton claimed to have gotten head from me in said locker room. I never stepped foot in that probably musty building my entire high school career and also never spoke a word to Carlton, never even shared a class with him. I'm not sure why Carlton devised this lie. I guess to get under Steven's skin. Mission accomplished. I felt like a slut when Steven interrogated me about it over the phone. He pressured me to quit cheering, but that's where I put my foot down. The day after Carlton's big lie, I heard football players gossiping about me in the gym while I headed outside to cheer practice. Word spread fast about me allegedly giving head to whoever wanted it. As I headed out the lunchroom doors with a friend one day, a guy tapped my friend on the shoulder to talk. When she joined me outside, she informed me, "He asked if you would give him head." Just one of several inquiries.

I felt so ashamed. I'd had protected sex with one guy within a monogamous relationship but somehow became the school whore. I even had to convince someone I considered a close friend that I hadn't given Carlton a blow job. Then came a rumor about Steven slapping me in the face in front of the gym. I was the school's collective punching bag. Meanwhile Steven got bragging rights by sharing our sexcapades, his reputation mostly unscathed. I get sad thinking about how hurt and confused I was. So young, so innocent. A piece of me hardened with the reality I needed to be more mindful of what I did with my body since the whole world felt entitled to policing it. I wasn't a dude. I couldn't just do *whatever* like boys could. If I wanted to be accepted by mainstream society, I simply couldn't be a roamer, a wanderer, a vagabond. I couldn't be a rolling stone.

Steven and I broke up the next spring, when we could no longer deny our incompatibility. Over the summer, I realized how isolated I had become. I had abandoned my friends for Steven. I decided to pick up my friendships where they had left off, make new friends, and focus on schoolwork and after school activities. I tried my best to conform to what society expected of "good" Black girls, including going to college. I graduated high school in 2005 near the top of my class and enrolled at the University of Georgia with a HOPE Scholarship covering my tuition and some smaller scholarships for living expenses. My freshman year, I made the Dean's List and got involved with organizations like the National Association of Black Journalists and the African Student Union. By most accounts, I was becoming a model citizen. She never told me this, but I know Mama was proud. She even sent me a basket filled with goodies and UGA merch. It seemed her hard work was paying off. Mama had fulfilled her role as a steady rock: a home where I knew I'd get my material needs met. What my dad thought of me I have no idea. We still weren't talking.

But things took a turn for the worse the summer after freshman year as I watched my grandmother wither away back home in our living room. Before I realized how bleak her prognosis was, I signed up for summer classes at the local college and got a job at Shane's Rib Shack. I spent so much time fulfilling my responsibilities I didn't remember to spend quality time with Grandma. I was in denial. Her cancer was untreatable. Our family surrounded her in the hospital the night she took her last breath, praying and singing "Amazing Grace." My grief manifested in my body when I returned to school. I resumed trying to be the "perfect" Black girl, taking a full load of classes and working part-time as a cashier at Kroger. I never anticipated my body giving out on me. Even though I knew about my dad's mystery illness, I didn't think of him as I got sick. Soon after moving back on campus, I caught what felt like a terrible cold, and it didn't go away. Then I started waking up to my hands burning and tingling, burning eyes, and a pink rash across my chest. My body hurt while walking around campus.

I became a staple at my university's health center, across the street from my apartment. I hobbled over there at least once a week. During a visit, one of their staff looked so concerned when I wasn't able to blow harder into a spirometer that I felt like I might be on death's doorstep. At another visit, a Black nurse gently counseled me after an OB-GYN discovered I had a bacterial infection, a small lump in my right breast, and elevated blood pressure: "You need to make sure you're staying on top of your health. Sometimes we Black women are really bad about that. We put everyone else's needs before our own." She made me feel like she truly cared. That small kindness was one bright moment in an otherwise dark period.

Despite having access to healthcare, no one could tell me exactly why my body was malfunctioning. My health was at an all-time low. I felt overwhelmed by life. I racked up speeding and parking tickets, maybe because my mind was foggy or maybe because cops are racist, or both. I withdrew from a required economics course, which I had never imagined having to do. Dating a cocky, country dude who fetishized light-skinned Black girls caused additional stress.

I worked nights and weekends at a Kroger near the county line, standing on my feet for hours as I scanned (sometimes heavy) items, tendered money, and bagged groceries. I got good reviews from secret shoppers who came through my line, which came with a five-dollar gift certificate. The staff was fairly diverse, but I didn't have any friends there. Most of the staff found me odd and acted passive-aggressive toward me. One of my few allies was a young Black guy who apparently hit on all UGA girls. I remember a superior making fun of my eyeliner and co-workers gossiping behind my back about how I acted slow but really wasn't. I think I was making mistakes, but my colleagues didn't know how to communicate with me.

The winter day I got called to the manager's office over the intercom, I felt particularly awful. My whole body ached as I scanned item after item on repeat. My line felt neverending. One customer misinterpreted my discomfort as aggression, and when the manager questioned me about the customer's complaint, I told him I would be putting in my resignation soon. It wasn't so much an act of defiance as an act of preservation. When I left his office, hot in the face, feeling worthless, I went to the breakroom to call Mama.

"I hate this job," I declared, voice cracking. I told her what had just happened between sniffles.

"I think you need to take a deep breath," Mama advised. "I know your college has a health center with counselors. You might want to try counseling. It's okay to need counseling." I still didn't think about Dad and whether his illness could be tied to mental health. I didn't have time to connect dots. I simply wanted to feel better.

I wiped away my tears and finished my shift. As soon as I got home, I Googled the benefits of therapy on my desktop. Of course I knew therapy existed, but I never really considered seeing a therapist myself. I saw therapy as something to watch on TV shows or something you only did when you hit rock bottom. My family would judge me if I got therapy, I thought. I never considered it an option for me. Still, I heeded Mama's advice, accepting her suggestion as permission, and went to an intake therapy appointment at the student health center. But I didn't hear back from them for months. Somehow I completed my fall semester courses with a decent showing. I was proud of myself for not giving up.

My health gradually improved the next semester. I can't pinpoint when I stopped being in constant physical and emotional pain. A few good things happened. I met a skinny jeans-wearing guy with a bald head and a mustache in the elevator of my apartment who soon became my boyfriend. We stayed together for the next three years and dated on and off for two more years. Our relationship was fun and lighthearted. He introduced me to indie music, house shows, and artsy queer and trans friends. I quit Kroger and got a job telefundraising for my school, then as a dorm desk assistant. I finally got assigned a therapist at the student health center. It was refreshing to share my feelings with a kind stranger. During our sessions, I didn't have any major breakthroughs but simply having someone in my corner put my mind at ease. A surgeon biopsied my breast lump, which turned out to be benign.

For the next two years, I successfully balanced school, work, volunteering, and freelance writing. I felt victorious in the face of the folks who treated me like a harlot back in tenth grade. I felt like I had a bright future, but then I had the misfortune of graduating in May 2009 at the height of the Great Recession. I couldn't find a "big girl job." As media outlets shuttered and shed employees, my journalism degree amounted to little. I tried out a graduate program in social work, what seemed like a practical, meaningful career, for a month or two. When I realized I wasn't sure about the program, I called Mama and Nicole crying. I quit grad school and worked part-time at different places in my college town, trying to figure out what I wanted to do with my life: a residential mental health facility, the local newspaper, a youth jobs program, the local library.

My family said I was lost, and my incessant partying didn't help their perception. On Friday nights, I would buy a pack of Camel Crush from the gas station and go bar hopping downtown or jump onto Georgia 316 to party in East Atlanta Village. I didn't care if I drove drunk. I drank in the car. When I told my therapist I smoked weed with my supervisor while on the clock, she said, "Sounds like you may not have that job for much longer." She was right, but I didn't care. I would just find some other soul-sucking, mind-numbing gig. I had given up on having a career and instead focused on soothing my emotional and mental pain by any means necessary, even if only temporarily. I felt left behind by college friends, unloved by family, and unwanted by the workforce. I felt like a good-for-nothing. I saw myself as a real waste of space. I rebelled against being a productive member of society because I felt forsaken by everybody and everything. I was merely existing.

I needed a change of scenery. Without informing my family, in 2010, I accepted an AmeriCorps volunteer position in a city I'd never even visited, Durham, North Carolina. The decision satiated my craving for novelty. Right before moving to Durham, I began dating a woman for the first time ever, a doctoral student in Columbia, South Carolina. A mutual friend from high school hooked us up. I wanted my first queer relationship to work out so badly, but it didn't. My mental state crumbled, and I ended up in a psychiatric ward for three days. Maybe I was lost like my family said. Maybe I was on my way to "getting sick" in the prime of my life just like my father.

✴

Erasmus was born an outsider, the "illegitimate" son of a priest and a physician's daughter. Still a boy when his parents died, Erasmus and his brother were sent to be trained as monks at a school where they suffered corporal punishment. Erasmus never fully got over the beatings. He then got sent to a monastery where he labeled his superiors as "barbaric" for discouraging his study of the classics. The young man was happy to escape the monastery by accepting the role of Latin secretary to a French bishop, but the position bored him.

He just couldn't seem to find his life path until embracing his fate as a wandering scholar.

Erasmus was never meant to stay in one place.

*

I hadn't heard from my dad for years, but through the grapevine, he found out I was living in North Carolina only two hours away from him. He asked to see me, so I told him we could meet at the Cracker Barrel near my apartment. I hadn't seen him since I was a preteen, but I'd always known I would have to see him eventually despite my resentment about his absence in my life. I figured seeing him wouldn't hurt. It was just something to do, and besides, I'd already hit the lowest of lows.

On a cool spring evening, I walked into the country store at the front of Cracker Barrel and saw my dad standing there, looking as if he'd been preserved in time. He looked youthful for sixty-three. He wore rose-tinted sunglasses, an ivy cap, a dark leather jacket over a red sweater, slacks, and alligator shoes. I looked casual next to him in my gray cable knit sweater, blue jeans, and a jacket. Still, I hadn't been this put together since before entering the mental hospital only a few months prior. We hugged awkwardly. He told me he liked my locs. After being seated and placing our order, small talk got deep pretty fast.

"You know why I didn't come around much when y'all were kids, don't you?" Dad asked, searching my eyes.

"Not really…" I replied, trying to keep a neutral face.

"Mannn, I was messed up back then. Serving in the army, getting caught up in drugs in the eighties…it all affected my mental health. I couldn't be there for y'all a lot of the time because I was sick."

I nibbled on a biscuit and nodded with understanding. So this is what Mama had been hiding all these years. Black families are infamous for sweeping mental health issues under the rug, and mine is no exception. I found Dad's confession refreshing, and of course I could empathize with him. Before I knew it, I was sharing something I hadn't told any other family member yet.

"Well, I can relate to that. I was actually in the psych ward about a month ago." I tried to speak nonchalantly, but it's hard to look nonplussed with a tear rolling down your cheek.

My father shook his head.

"Wow, I'm sorry to hear that. I hope I didn't pass my craziness down to you." I detected sadness in his tone.

Something shifted that night. We realized we weren't just father and daughter; we were both merely humans struggling with the human condition. Mental illness had forged a bond between us. By speaking with each other about it, we were breaking generational curses. I took pictures of Dad with my digital camera, and we got the cashier to take our picture together before parting, to send to Nicole and Mama later. To my left in the photo, Dad is giving a peace sign.

A few months later on Mother's Day weekend, I pulled up to Baccarat Road in Kelford. The old schoolhouse was still there behind Grandma E's trailer but no longer served as a club nor anything else. She stopped running the club with her husband, Mr. Bobby, when he began showing signs of dementia (he died soon after that trip). When I visited with her, I found out no one goes in there anymore, and she would like to see it bulldozed.

I kicked it with my dad. The steps to Dad's front porch were broken but usable. The living room's wood paneling and carpet looked dated yet exuded a certain charm. His boxing poster was still on the wall.

In the living room, we caught up on lost years. He told me my hair reminded him of his favorite musician, Tracy Chapman. He told me about the mental health support groups he participates in at the Veteran Affairs Hospital and gave me a bunch of literature from them. He told me he met my mother working as her supervisor at a New York State mental hospital and wants to write a book about being on both sides of the mental health system. He showed me his guitars. He showed me a photo of his mixed-race daughter I had only heard rumors about. He talked about how he stays in Kelford to keep an eye on my grandmother but dreams of living in New Orleans. He tried to teach me how to drive a stick in his red Mustang with the nickname "D. Black" in silver letters above the handles. He took me with him to collect on a gambling debt and to a fight party, where I embarrassed him by bumming a cigarette (he thought it made him look broke and made the guy take his money). He drove me an hour away to Greenville to eat at Red Lobster. Before we ate, he stopped by Men's Wearhouse, where the saleswoman knew him by name. Driving home from Greenville, he spoke about when he got sick.

"One afternoon, I decided to snort as much coke as I could. I was in my forties, doing well in my career, but I couldn't keep my nose clean. It was the eighties. Everyone was getting high," my father explained. "That day, I did so much coke, I thought I was having a heart attack. Somehow, I drove myself to the hospital. My doctor told me he used to do coke, so he knew personally that I could've died that day. I haven't done drugs or alcohol since." Upon getting out of the hospital, he went to rehab, retired early, and moved back home.

As we got closer to his trailer, my dad told me he dreamed of starting a business on the family land with his youngest child. Me. "Wouldn't that be something?" he asked. He didn't specify what type of business, but I secretly envisioned us preserving the schoolhouse and running it as a museum. Later, he texted my mother, thanking her for doing such a good job raising his daughters. I figured he must be overwhelmed by emotion to send such an uncharacteristic text. It felt surreal when Mama texted back, "You're welcome." Finally, my parents getting along. It only took a few decades.

We never started that business, never even talked about it again. I guess there's still time, but I'm still not close to my dad, who's in his seventies now. We never talk on the phone. I see him during special occasions, like our family reunion the summer of 2019 and his joint birthday party with Grandma E in January 2023. I feel obligated to show up because Dad and Grandma E aren't getting any younger. I want them to know I care, even if we're not tight. Dad and I are always civil to each other, but we don't go deep like we did at Cracker Barrel. Maybe the timing hasn't been right. Maybe I still want a happy ending even if I know those usually only happen in Disney movies.

Sometimes I feel like too many bridges have burned between us. My dad never fully embraced playing a fatherly role in my life, and now it feels too late for him to try. He chose his path, and I chose mine. I don't know how to be a daughter to someone who doesn't know how to father me. But despite the gulf between us, we'll always have things in common. I think my father and I are both rolling stones at heart. We're unpredictable and mercurial. We're both stubborn as mules.

On the other hand, I think the COVID-19 pandemic has slowed us both down a bit. We're both in stable, long-term relationships and live fairly quiet, simple lives. Gathering moss as we stay in one place. Mostly. In the next phase of my life, I want to travel more beyond the U.S. So far I've made it to Cape Town, South Africa, and Vancouver, Canada. I want to see the rest of Canada and visit as many African countries as possible, and Mexico, Cuba, Thailand, the Netherlands, Ireland, England, and wherever else the wind blows me. Jojo and I are already family planning, and I hope our future kid can see the world with us. A little moss never hurt a stone.

Farmers' Alliance Hall in Hog Hummock, Sapelo Island, Georgia. Built circa 1929.

A Brush with Magic
or an Ode to Mrs. Cornelia

CORNELIA WALKER BAILEY OF SAPELO ISLAND, Georgia died as a toddler—but got brought back to life.

After the island carpenter had already built her pine box casket, her aunt packed garlic into her nose. Just like that, the small child awoke. From then on, the community thought the girl possessed special powers. Elders or "bin yahs" didn't often talk to young people—but she was the one exception. They flocked to the girl to understand where she'd been. She existed between two worlds: Earth and the other side.

Mrs. Cornelia believed in magic. In her 2000 memoir, co-authored with Christena Bledsoe, *God, Dr. Buzzard, and the Bolito Man: A Saltwater Geechee Talks about Life on Sapelo Island*, she wrote, "Back in the 1940s when I was growing up, it was part of everyday life [over here on Sapelo Island] to believe in magic and signs and spirits. My family absolutely believed. That's right. The spirits were always in our lives. Always. People talked to the spirits and accused them of playing tricks and being full of mischief."

Mrs. Cornelia died (again) at age seventy-two in 2017 but not before leaving an indelible mark on the world. Everyone in McIntosh County knew Mrs. Cornelia, including my mom who grew up across the river from Sapelo in the small city of Darien and raised me and my siblings in nearby Brunswick. When I showed Mama a book I got for sale from Powell's Books in 2018, *Sapelo's People: A Long Walk into Freedom* (1994) by William S. McFeely, the first thing she asked was, "Do they talk about Mrs. Cornelia Bailey?" The island's resident griot—the community oral historian and storyteller, a tradition brought to coastal Georgia by enslaved West Africans who revered this role—Mrs. Cornelia was a gatekeeper who had every right to be one, but she also graciously shared her magic. When McFeely embarked on his research, meeting with Mrs. Cornelia was one of his first stops. Upon leaving her job with the State of Georgia in the 1970s, she became a full-time activist as a founder of Hog Hammock Community Foundation in 1976, Sapelo Island Cultural and Revitalization Society or SICARS in 1993, and the nonprofit Save Our Land Ourself (now known as Save Our Legacy Ourself or SOLO) in 2010. She specialized in bringing people together. On weekends, Sapelonians and their mainland kin would gather at her home to smoke, drink, flirt, and party, even ministers and deacons. One of her primary collaborators, UGA, suggested putting up a plaque in her honor when she died. Her son, Maurice Bailey, didn't think she would like that since she was so action-oriented. He convinced them to instead establish the Cornelia Walker Bailey Program on Land and Agriculture, of which he is a co-director.

According to Maurice, "People always told her all the history and stories. She could remember all that stuff. It was the 1990s before she started writing stuff down. She could recite everybody's birthday, who was related, who was married to who, how many kids they had, where they lived, et cetera. She was that person in the community everybody turned to for information and advice because they trusted whatever she said. She had this ability to make things happen."

I will never get to meet Mrs. Cornelia in the flesh but feel a kinship with her anyway. I, too, seek to tell and preserve the story of my roots on Georgia's coast and to bring people together to celebrate our culture. After reading McFeely's book, I dreamed of walking in Mrs. Cornelia's shoes and one day seeing the place she called home. As a kid, I'd always gazed with curiosity at the sign pointing to Sapelo standing next to my church. Writing this book finally pushed me to see what lies beyond the sign. Time to look for Mrs. Cornelia. Since she believed in magic, I knew her spirit must still be there presiding over the island's affairs.

Googling around led me to Maurice, a fifty-three-year-old former welder, community activist, and founder/CEO of SOLO, which is dedicated to preserving the culture, heritage, and traditions of Sapelo's Gullah Geechee people, descendants of enslaved West Africans. The youngest of Mrs. Cornelia's six children (his mother also fostered countless children with behavioral issues sent to her from the mainland), Maurice tends her flame for community service. I reached out to him online in summer 2022. After chatting for a few weeks, I invited him to visit my suburban Atlanta home when he would be in town for an event in late July.

When Maurice stopped by my house, I opened the door to a stout, glasses-wearing man of average height wearing a baseball cap. Maurice is taking on the arduous task of holding on to what his mother and other ancestors built. When I first spoke with him over the phone, he mentioned how Sapelo's Black residents rarely gain anything from sharing their stories with the outside world. Not a small number of white writers and academics charge themselves with uncovering the history and culture; a culture swiftly slipping through Maurice's fingers as Sapelonians die or move away and descendants sell or lose ancestral land. Land theft has been happening for decades but has intensified within the past decade.

Chatting with me and Jojo in his warm twang over a cup of coffee on our screened-in back porch, he expressed frustration with white people perpetually claiming the island for themselves since the 1700s. Much of the land formerly owned by descendants of the four hundred enslaved West Africans—forty-four original families who labored in Sapelo—is now in white hands. Black folks there began purchasing land shortly after slavery ended. Once home to more than a dozen Black communities, now only Hog Hammock, or Hog Hummock as descendants call it, remains. A long line of wealthy white men owned Sapelo, including slave masters, dictating how the island ran even after Black folks could buy land. In 1969 and 1976, the widow of its last owner, tobacco heir Richard J. Reynolds, Jr., sold it for research purposes to the State of Georgia, which owns nearly all the island's 16,500 acres—except for Hog Hummock's 434 acres. The state, largely run by white Republicans, is now seen as the primary caretaker and steward of the land. Maurice is tired of white folks controlling Sapelo's narrative. As he spoke, I felt frustrated for him. I didn't want to be grouped in with white storytellers who believe their positionality bestows authority upon them. My academic training and writing experience is no match for Maurice's ancestral knowledge. After he left my home, I resolved to approach my trip to Sapelo and subsequent writings with humility and empathy. I would look to the remaining Black folks in Sapelo as survivors, not subjects.

I suppose my spouse, Jojo, and I didn't come off as serial killers because when I asked if he would give us a tour of the island, he agreed to host us Labor Day weekend.

The night before we arrived, Maurice called to say he was stuck in South Carolina due to car trouble so wouldn't be on the island to greet us. Fancying ourselves self-sufficient, we didn't fret over this news. I felt confident enough as Jojo and I drove through drizzly weather from our hotel in Brunswick to catch the Friday 8:30 a.m. ferry to Sapelo from the Meridian dock, only a few miles from my childhood church. We crept up to the dock's crowded parking lot, unsure of what to do and where to go. We lugged our suitcases and cooler down a surprisingly long road, and were eventually met by a young Black man with a clipboard working for the ferry's operator, the Georgia Department of Natural Resources. To visit Sapelo, you must be on their list, a restriction put in place to protect the island's delicate ecosystem and purportedly also the descendants. We gave our names to the worker who turned out to be Maurice's nephew. When he asked us each for a five-dollar fee, something we'd known about in advance, my face flushed with embarrassment: We had forgotten to bring cash. We stood off to the side as he checked in other riders. I felt like an idiot. A kind stranger agreed to spot us the cash if we sent him the money on Cash App. I made sure to send him a little extra.

Rushing onto the modest white ferry, we stuck out like sore thumbs. Aside from a few workers, we were the only Black folks on the ferry, Katie Underwood, named after Sapelo's legendary midwife (1884-1977), a daughter of freedmen, who, according to local legend, never lost a baby. I'd anticipated this, being the only Black visitors, yet the scene cloaked me in unease. I eyeballed my fellow riders with a dose of suspicion as we laid our rain jackets down on a wet bench to sit. From my point of view, the ills of white supremacy were responsible for Black people's strife in Sapelo. Because of white developers conspiring with white officials to grab land, Sapelo's status as a majority-Black island is in danger. Population statistics vary; one source places the population at fifty-three percent Black with one hundred ninety-five residents total while another cites 54.2 percent Black with two hundred-eight residents total.

Also at stake is Hog Hummock's standing as one of the last intact Gullah Geechee communities in the United States. Gullah Geechee describes a set of traditions that developed among enslaved West Africans and their descendants in insulated sea islands and hamlets along the Southeastern coast. Blending practices from their native land and their new home, they created their own distinct arts, language, food, and spirituality. Many Black folks from Sapelo call themselves "Saltwater Geechees" to distinguish themselves from "Freshwater Geechees" on the mainland.

I had no idea about the significance of Sapelo and its Gullah Geechee culture until I noticed them featured in big name publications as an adult. This seems to be a common narrative among Black people from coastal Georgia: not knowing how important Sapelo is to African American history and culture until later in life. It seems the island's story got buried by local African Americans who wanted to move away from the old ways Sapelo represented—living off the land in an all-Black community—to living in integrated neighborhoods near commerce and industry, which they saw as progress. Black folks after Mrs. Cornelia's generation probably deemed the island's history unremarkable and unworthy of being passed down. The State of Georgia prioritizes using the island's resources over preserving its indigenous African land and culture, and thus, the story didn't make it into our textbooks. Even Maurice didn't begin identifying as

Geechee until the term and its meaning became more well-known in the mid-1980s, his early adulthood (he sees Geechee as the same thing as Gullah—some distinguish between the two, claiming the Gullah hail from the Carolinas and the Geechee from Georgia and Florida). Before then, he only knew of himself as a "Sapelonian," what folks called him on the mainland.

Later, during our Saturday tour, Maurice would tell me, "People didn't know our strength living on Sapelo. We didn't know we were special Black people. We didn't know we were Geechee people. We didn't know our connection to African and Muslim traditions. We didn't know years ago that everybody would be focused on us, our culture, and our intellectual property. We were just living our life. We didn't cherish those things, so a lot of it got lost." On the boat, I felt grateful to be headed to this special place that was kept a secret from me during childhood.

Right before the Katie Underwood docked, an older white woman with a scattering of tattoos, long white hair, and flowy clothes approached us. In a soft, raspy voice, she told us her name was Ruth. Maurice had asked her to drive us to his place in Hog Hummock. We followed her through the dock's parking lot, buzzing with workers and tourists, to an old white van with taped up windows bearing the name and acronym of Maurice's organization and its motto, "Honoring the past & protecting the future." In a nod to SOLO's mission, a colorful Sankofa bird graced the van. Originating with Ghana's Akan tribe, Sankofa means, "It is not taboo to fetch what is at risk of being left behind." Two older white men joined us, on their way to Maurice's convenience store—the sole store on the island—to uninstall a broken ATM machine that had been there for years.

As we drove out the parking lot, we passed a long line of cars. Ruth told us some of them were abandoned, while others belonged to residents. She told us she worked at Maurice's store. We creaked along a one-lane road in the hot van past pine trees, live oaks, and saw palmetto—and the very occasional vehicle. After about ten minutes, we were welcomed by a large, weathered sign. Underneath a drawing of a little house reminiscent of the ones surrounding us, it read, "Historic Hog Hammock Community established circa 1857, 434 acres, pop. 70." Below this read, "Home of Allen Bailey – Atlanta Falcons," a homage to Maurice's NFL football player cousin, the island's most famous native next to Mrs. Cornelia. Humble old bungalows contrasted starkly with large, newer homes on stilts. Pavement turned into dirt. We passed Maurice's store, a church, another sign commemorating Allen's time with the Kansas City Chiefs.

"Here we are," Ruth said as we pulled in front of a duplex slightly raised above the ground with a red metal roof. We got out without any fanfare. She drove off to start her shift.

Jojo and I carried our things through the muddy front yard to the door on the left, finding it unlocked (a sign on the door to the right warned us not to enter). A group of workers stayed in the guesthouse right before us, and Maurice, stuck in South Carolina, hadn't been able to clean before we arrived. The air conditioning unit hummed as we explored our accommodations. On the walls were a map of Sapelo, a drawing of Mrs. Cornelia, and photos of Maurice working the land alongside others. The scent of men who spent their days toiling in the scorching sun wafted through the air. They had left a plate of food in the microwave and a mountain of red plastic cups in the sink. Window screens were no match for the bugs, abundant after days of heavy rain. I could sense Jojo's discomfort, increasing my own through osmosis. We decided to get some fresh air on the detached porch.

The porch was slightly taller than the roof with a skinny metal slide attached. From it, a Juneteenth flag flew proudly, red and blue with a white star in the middle. We took in Maurice's yard, a muddy casualty of flooding when it rains hard or the tide is high: its tiny dwellings with metal roofs, cars underneath metal awnings, two buses, a red tractor, and several golf carts. I fiddled with my phone to see if it would pick up Wi-Fi from the house because I couldn't get service otherwise.

An ache radiated out from the back of my neck. Sweat permeated my T-shirt. Modern-day amenities felt lightyears away. Thick, humid heat and swarms of mosquitoes crawled over my skin, enveloping me in aggravation. I found little solace looking out at an endless canopy of trees and miles of blue skies painted with fluffy clouds. Jojo's anxiety was palpable. We sucked on our vape pen, slathered on bug spray to little effect, and spoke to each other in irritated tones. The vape pen couldn't remedy my flustered state, nor could the thrill of the boat, having just seen dolphins leap out the Doboy Sound and egrets bob in the marshes. The presence of Jojo, around whom I typically feel calm and safe, provided no consolation. Had I made a mistake by coming here? For weeks planning this trip, I thought stepping foot on this land would instantly feel like a homecoming.

Instead, I felt out of my element. Like a complete foreigner, a little like a fraud. I had dreamed of Sapelo as if it were a promised land, as if it would feel holy soon as I touched down. Now I wondered whether I could make it through one night there. Black folks who leave here might be on to something, I thought. Maybe I was chasing an illusion.

My initial visions of Sapelo were informed by the writings of white folks, such as the late historian McFeely. These people write with authority about Bilali Muhammed—Maurice's ancestor—the enslaved African from Guinea appointed to be a slave driver who brought Islam to Sapelo, making him one of the first Muslims in the U.S.; about how enslaved Africans there had more freedom than those on the mainland, and about how the island's remoteness allowed its Black residents to retain elements of their West African culture. After reading *Sapelo's People*, I built the island up in my head to be some kind of Mecca, a place of birthright for African Americans. Whenever someone mentioned Sapelo, I proudly proclaimed my people were from near there.

McFeely's words were my first introduction to the legendary Mrs. Cornelia. The historian first met her when she spoke to his students about Sapelo's history and took them oystering and fishing the next day. He writes of her serving as the island's voting registrar and driving children on a bus to catch the ferry to attend school (Sapelo's K-8 school closed in 1978 and now serves as the public library). He describes her as "proud and handsome, the island's chronicler and its most ardent, outspoken champion," "keeper of the kingdom," and "angry and articulate." He goes on, "'Take a number and get in line' is her breezy, caustic advice in the face of the storming of Sapelo by curiosity seekers ranging from academic African linguists to real estate predators." McFeely paints a picture of the benevolent gatekeeper.

McFeely gained access to the island via my predominantly white alma mater, UGA, as a professor in their history department, retiring a decade before I took classes there as a history minor. UGA operates a 1,500-acre marine institute on the south end of the island next to the Reynolds Mansion, a tabby relic of the island's plantation past built by enslaved people for their "master," Thomas Spalding, who owned the island. (Tabby concrete, made from burned oyster shells turned into lime mixed with ash, sand, and water, has long been a popular building material on Georgia's coast, likely transported here in the 1500s from Africa's west coast.) The mansion is now a popular wedding venue. McFeely yearned to know more about the lives of the Black service workers employed by UGA and the mansion, which he refers to as the "big house," and where they lived. "I was curious. I wanted to know the Hog Hammock people in their own world, to meet them in a place that was not alien to us both. I knew that I wanted to put the south end behind me," he writes.

Like any sound scholar (including myself), McFeely questions whether he is a good fit for researching his topic of choice: "Will I be just one more intruder on the island's fierce, frightened privacy?" The historian had been cautioned by "good liberals at the wheel" that outsiders weren't welcome in Hog Hummock. He tells the story of one psychologist who purportedly became so intimate with the community while doing a demographic study she vowed to write about them only when they are dead: "She senses a fear, not a mere reluctance, among members of the Hog Hammock community that they will be violated, displaced, by exposure, by the telling of their stories." McFeely muses on whether he's just another intruder but never really answers the question, only posing new ones: "Isn't the opposite of intrusive exploitation sometimes self-protective reticence? Can't silence be both patronizing and wrong? If averting the eye of the privileged—privileged with education and practice in writing—were to be the only action taken in such situations, wouldn't the story of Sapelo's people and others similarly valuable be lost?" He posits "some of the most sensitive renderings that exist of Southern life" wouldn't have been created without outsiders, citing two white men's nonfiction: *Nets & Doors: Shrimping in Southern Waters* (1989) and *Oystering: A Way of Life* (1983) by UGA-educated author and photographer Jack Leigh and the oral history *All God's Dangers: The Life of Nate Shaw* (1974) about a Black sharecropper imprisoned for defending his neighbor's crop from white deputies, written by Harvard-educated historian Theodore Rosengarten. Ultimately, he resolves to pay his subjects "honorable attention," then moves to the next chapter.

I wonder if he ever bothered to ask Geechee folks in Sapelo whether they wanted to record and document their stories themselves. Surely he had access to resources that could have been used for this purpose. Of course academia doesn't view building mutually beneficial relationships with communities as as valuable as writing books about them. But with a Pulitzer Prize under his belt and his white cishet male protection, McFeely could have probably gotten away with subverting academic research norms. It's disappointing when those with extreme privilege and also an understanding of oppression refuse to transform "the way things have always been" to lift up the most oppressed.

Don't get me wrong: I'm grateful to have discovered McFeely's book because it increased what I knew of Sapelo's culture and history. I imagine the historian as a noble man, especially given his contributions to forming Yale's African American studies department in the 1970s. But I don't agree with his failure to truly "pass the mic," nor with how he skims over the destruction wrought by systemic racism in Sapelo. He skips right to the magic of African worldbuilding. The professor deemed himself deserving of telling this story simply because he was endorsed by the right, white institutions. I traveled to Sapelo vowing to be different from him.

Still, I felt like as much of an outsider as McFeely once I arrived in Sapelo. I worried my narrative would be as superficial and unfamiliar as any white academic's. Getting the story wrong or leaving out critical parts à la McFeely could ultimately do more harm than good. I worried my engagement with the people of Sapelo would be transactional instead of relational and that I might not be compelled to return after this visit. Maybe I wasn't even worthy of Maurice's invitation. I wondered why I felt so much like an outsider when Mama worked in Sapelo as a home healthcare nurse in the early 1990s and my relatives and their resting places were just on the other side of the Doboy Sound. I had hoped my proximity would infuse my words with more respect, regard, and authenticity than the writers who came before me. Best case scenario, my words would inspire action to protect Geechee people, culture, and land (in contrast, McFeely's book affected no apparent material gains in the lives of Sapelonians). I knew I needed to lean into my discomfort on the island if this was my endgame.

"Let's check out the store," I beckoned to Jojo after surveying Maurice's backyard. Trekking down a dirt road to the store, white men in a big truck splashed mud until passing us while white boys whizzed by on a golf cart. It's one thing to see gentrification in a city, quite another to see it somewhere remote. I'm not even sure it can be called gentrification since the term connotes an urban area. It's displacement for sure. Growing up in Sapelo, Maurice rarely saw white people; now white people are surprised to see *him* on the island. In 1983, the State of Georgia pledged to help keep the land in descendants' hands through the creation of the Sapelo Island Heritage Authority but is failing to fulfill its promise. When a piece of land in Sapelo is sold, the authority is supposed to acquire it for the descendants' benefit but instead has been enabling it to be bought by outsiders. The state doesn't properly fund the entity nor consult with descendants about the composition of the board.

We walked past fields of sugarcane and red peas, a row of beehives, and St. Luke Baptist Church, one of two active houses of worship on the island, on our way to the store. I perked up at these emblems of resilience. Painted haint blue, a Gullah Geechee tradition—historically, they painted their homes light blue to keep haints or ghosts from entering—the store donned a mural of a man wearing a cowboy hat and glasses (presumably Maurice) wielding a white sheet concealing the body of a Black man (presumably an ancestor) next to a Sankofa bird and the phrase, "The Spirit of Sapelo." There were signs promoting SOLO, their Geechee red peas project, and a fishing tournament. In front of raised garden beds, a yard sign celebrated the high school graduation of the worker we met at the ferry. This was clearly the community hub.

I waved to our fellow van passengers as we walked past them on the store's porch drinking beer. Inside, a pair of women from a tour bus outside bought the last can of bug spray. We browsed the small but well-stocked store. I grappled with whether I deserved a late morning ice cream, ultimately deciding against it. I picked out a blue "Hog Hammock" T-shirt bearing an image of a hog reading in a hammock with moss overhead. Jojo picked out the green version of this irresistible shirt. Then we chatted with Ruth at the cash register. I sat my tiny recorder on the counter.

I told Ruth about my quest to write a book recovering Black history in coastal Georgia while uncovering my relationship to it. She fell in love with the area and its "colorful history" while on vacation at the start of the pandemic, settling down in McIntosh after getting injured on said vacation. While volunteering for a white-led education, outreach, and research nonprofit in Sapelo, she fell in love with the Gullah Geechee culture and learned of the store assistant gig. The job gives her a front row seat to comings and goings on the island and "intriguing" community meetings at the church across the way. After one meeting, a lady came into the store declaring her need for a stiff drink.

A former resident of Hawaii, Ruth said she didn't want what happened there to happen in Sapelo. I resisted the urge to furrow my brows. What happened and is still happening in Hawaii—tourists driving up the cost of living, ruining the environment, and disrespecting the Indigenous culture—is already in motion in Sapelo and has been for decades. I willed my eyes not to roll as she explained being born in Latin America and thus always rooting for the "underdog or the ethnic people."

"That's what pulls me," Ruth said. "I like culture and people, that kind of stuff...I understand that years ago, people used to meet here. This was a bar right behind me. There was a B & B. This building behind me belonged to...Corneeeliaaa Bailey, Maurice's mom."

Ruth's voice drifted far away as she pointed to a 2008 *New York Times* article on the opposite wall titled, "A Georgia Community With an African Feel Fights a Wave of Change" (penned by the non-Black reporter Shaila Dewan who got married at Sapelo's "big house"). It includes a photo of Mrs. Cornelia cradling her grandson as he sucks his thumb.

"You want to read about her right there and actually Google her. This was her place, and this was lively. People would meet—Black, white, whatever—they would meet here, and they would party, and they would hang out and BBQ, whatever, and...it's not happening anymore. Maurice hasn't brought it back that way. He's very private."

Ruth learned more about Sapelo from Maurice's relatives than from him. He would show and tell me only what *he* wanted to show and tell me, she said.

"Maybe it's because I'm white he doesn't speak much to me. Maybe he'll be different with you, I don't know...and I respect that absolutely," Ruth wondered aloud.

"I feel like there's so many outsiders coming in..." I remarked, gently defending this man I barely knew.

"Yes, and I don't blame him at all because I've seen it happen, so I truly understand that, and I really don't want to step on his toes because

I really do like him, and I respect what he's trying to do in his own way."

"I'm thankful for what he's doing. Seems like a lot of people are supporting."

Ruth proceeded to laud Maurice's new tractor and his farming, mentioning she wanted to help with it in the future because of her family's background in horticulture. Still, she spoke as if she thought he could be doing more for the island. For her, that looks like bringing more people into the mix and being less of a gatekeeper. Did she expect Maurice to run himself ragged molding Hog Hummock into what others want it to be?

"You've gotta see the island…you got a map?" Ruth inquired.

She handed each of us a map, pointing out landmarks. She urged us to visit Cabretta Beach to see sea turtles hatch, despite it being less accessible than the other beach Nanny Goat. She got a call on her cell from Maurice, surprising her because she rarely got service in the store. When she handed me the phone, Maurice apologized for not being there and asked if we could pick him up from the ferry while dropping Ruth off around 4 p.m.

Jojo and I left the store to explore a little, walking toward the office of the nonprofit SICARS, a white-shingled bungalow with rocking chairs on its large porch, and the public library, a blue manufactured home with white accents. Both were closed that day.

"So…if Ruth is so against displacement, why did she live in Hawaii? Natives there have been begging outsiders to stay away for years," I wondered aloud.

"Yeah, she's a real trip…typical white liberal," Jojo replied.

"I mean, she was speaking as if she knows better than Maurice what the island needs. I hate when white people do that. At least she gave us a ride and these handy dandy maps…"

"She sure did. I guess Ruth is our new bestie."

"I guess so. Hey, wanna try out those rocking chairs?"

We walked up to SICARS porch and rocked away, swatting at bugs with our maps and digesting our new surroundings.

I rolled off the couch as my phone's alarm clock went off. Time to pick up Maurice. After leaving the rocking chairs, we had looked for Cabretta Beach in the SOLO van without any luck, headed back to Maurice's place, ate heated up frozen foods, and watched a docuseries about Woodstock, to which I had dozed off. Rolling up to the store in the van, we spotted Ruth leaning into a truck window about to catch a ride to the dock. We scooped her up, deposited her at the dock, and waited for a few minutes until seeing Maurice walk toward us with his hands full of groceries. I tried to navigate the road like a pro, no easy feat without a passing lane. Maurice said he wasn't used to riding in the backseat. When we told him about our fruitless sojourn to Cabretta Beach initiated by Ruth, he sighed deeply. We could also see sea turtles hatch at Nanny Goat, he said. Back at his place, he jumped to cleaning the guest house, then cooking chicken on the front porch grill. We all chatted until he sent me and Jojo to pick up his friend, Adé, from the last ferry of the day.

Adé and his co-worker, Grace, were on the island to prepare for Sapelo Cultural Day, held each October at the Farmers' Alliance building. Within a few minutes, we learned they worked for Project South, an Atlanta movement organization both my wife and I have been involved with on and off throughout the years. I attended their popular education program, University Sin Fronteras, in 2013 and their 2019 Southern Movement Assembly in Hazlehurst, Mississippi. We dropped them off at their lodging, a house owned by Abraham Baldwin Agricultural College, only to pick them up a few hours later when it got dark. We were on our way to hang out at Maurice's place. A geography professor who researches racial coastal formation in Sapelo also joined us. That night, things flowed naturally between us all. We made for an eclectic crew: a Sapelonian activist, a Black writer from coastal Georgia, a Rwandese American who trains community organizations, a Black educator from Atlanta, a biracial Black organizer from Miami, and a Southern white academic. It was as if the universe conspired for us to be together at the same time and the same place. The word "kismet" comes to mind. We were fellowshiping in a way that Ruth claimed no longer happens on the island.

"So you're from Brunswick, eh? Man...y'all got it going on," Adé remarked as the group sat around Maurice's porch. "Y'all were some of the only ones able to hold white murderers accountable with Ahmaud Arbery's case. There's something special about y'all."

"Funny you say that. Growing up, I sure didn't think we were anything special. I wanted to get away from Brunswick as soon as possible," I responded, taking a sip of my mixed drink.

"And look at you now, back in good ol' coastal Georgia. I love coming down here whenever I can. It's like a second home. Y'all Gullah Geechee folks are some powerful people."

Jojo chimed in. "Agreed. But it's wild because Neesha's family won't even claim Gullah Geechee. I've heard her mom say more than once, 'We're not Gullah Geechee.' But they fit all the criteria."

"Are you serious?" Adé asked. He shook his head. "When people won't even claim what they really are...that's deep."

"Yeah...I think it's because when she was growing up, being Geechee was not a cool thing to be," I explained. "It was stigmatized back then."

"I guess that makes sense. Maurice tells me you're a journalist, and you're here because you're writing a book?"

"Yep. I'm writing all about how I never knew the cultural and historical significance of where I lived growing up and my journey to reclaiming my ancestors' culture."

"Wow…do you know how big of a deal that is? How many other Black women from around here have gotten a book published?"

"Not many…" My chest swelled with pride (and booze).

"Exactly. You should be proud of yourself. So should your family. Maybe it will encourage them to claim their Gullah Geechee roots."

"Maybe."

We eventually migrated to the tall porch. We were up there for hours, eating, making connections, getting to know each other, yelling about electoral politics. Usually, I would've been bothered by the bug spray stain on my shirt, but I didn't care to change. I lived in the moment, basking in the gallons of stars one can't see in the city, watching the occasional plane go by. Adé, Grace, Jojo, and I realized we were friends with several of the same people through movement work. We also found out the professor, who thoroughly entertained us when he opened a beer with a porch railing, is a colleague of my wife's former professor and mentor. All of us cackled at the expense of Herschel Walker and his abysmal run for U.S. senator. My anxiety about surviving in Sapelo melted away.

Our get together wound down around midnight. Jojo, Grace, Adé, and I were sitting in the guest house living room when Adé asked if I had ever heard of the Darien Insurrection. I had never met anyone else who knew about the insurrection, and I told him so. During the 1899 insurrection, Darien's Black population took up arms to successfully defend a Black man from being lynched after he was wrongfully accused of raping a white woman. We chatted about the event excitedly. Black history nerd heaven.

"Did you know that after the insurrection, they sent guns in coffins to the AUC (Atlanta University Center) to defend themselves during Atlanta's 1906 race riot?" Adé asked.

I had never heard this despite living in or near Atlanta for a decade. I didn't even know much about the Atlanta Race Massacre, one of the city's most horrific massacres spurred by the alleged rapes of four white women by Black men in September 1906. Atlanta does a damn good job of hiding its long history of racial terror and Black resistance by pretending it's always been "too busy to hate." The massacre resulted in up to one-hundred African Americans being killed by white vigilantes, who took to the streets in thousands, injuring or murdering every African American in sight. Black people from outside the city smuggled guns to Atlanta's Black residents by concealing them in caskets and soiled laundry. According to Adé, some of those firearms came from Darien. It seems Black folks from Georgia's coast to its capital have always had each other's backs. We may live in different places, yet we share an irrevocable bond. This is why I believe in Black people telling Black stories—and why I dared to write this essay.

I felt grateful as I headed to bed. This was the magic I'd been waiting for.

Our tour started the next morning at 9 a.m. I'm not a morning person, especially after a night of drinking, but I pushed aside grouchiness as we loaded into the van. For the next few hours, Jojo and I entered Maurice's world, learning of his struggle to protect an island so many outsiders want to claim without pouring back into it. Maurice started giving tours in the 1990s when he noticed tours guided by the state left out the story of Sapelo's African Americans but doesn't give many tours nowadays due to the time-consuming work of running SOLO.

Driving us around Hog Hummock, he pointed out houses in disrepair, many of them abandoned by descendants. At the time of our visit, he said there were twenty-seven descendants left on the island ranging from age two to eighty-two.

The land grab intensified around 2016, Maurice says, with less than two hundred acres of the community now owned by descendants: "It's really out of control right now. This is a critical point. If we don't do something right now, we're going to lose more people and more land. The non-descendants are just stacking the deck, working with their politician buddies in the 'good ol' boy' system. Things are constantly being changed because they know we're fighting and will eventually win our fight. They've made it clear once you become a property owner, you have as many rights as descendants. Before we had certain rights that non-descendants didn't."

Land in Sapelo is valuable to wealthy white people because of the isolation and the beaches, Maurice says—they see it as their own "elite resort plantation" only their family and friends can access by putting their name on the ferry list, which acts as a sort of gate. These folks demand the ferry run on holidays so people can visit them. They want Sapelo to revolve around their comfort. They don't care whether descendants maintain their connection with ancestral land. They don't care if one day nobody's left on the island who remembers the lives of Black Sapelonians used to revolve around the Farmers' Alliance—the selling, trading, learning, socializing, celebrating, and dancing. Or how families split up their children between the island's two churches to increase their chances when it came time to court. Or how white folks ran them out of Raccoon Bluff by building a new First African Baptist Church in Hog Hummock and plotted to relocate them to the mainland until Mrs. Cornelia found out.

They prefer a Sapelo where the only Black people are ghosts.

As Maurice said, the descendants are fighting mightily to keep Sapelo Geechee. Over the past decade, they've filed several lawsuits to counter exorbitant property taxes and inadequate public services. A few months before my visit, fifty-seven descendants settled with McIntosh County who agreed to provide two million dollars in damages, quarterly road maintenance, a reduced solid waste fee, an emergency medical truck, a fire truck and volunteer firefighter training, a three-year property tax freeze, and potentially a helicopter landing area. But Maurice doesn't really see these lawsuits as wins, even though most outsiders do. He believes their intention is financial gain for individuals and not for the community. Public services were already in place, he says, but the county and state pulled back on them once the lawsuits began. According to him, some people who tried to join these lawsuits don't live in Sapelo and have never lived there. On the other hand, I know descendants who live off-island, or "abroad" as Maurice calls it, but still deeply identify with their ancestral home and would probably argue they deserve to be plaintiffs. Who has the right to call themselves a Sapelonian and lay claim to the land is a complicated and nuanced matter of which I am unqualified to weigh in.

Only Sapelonians can be buried in Behavior Cemetery, the island's sole active cemetery founded before the Civil War and located in what used to be a Black settlement, the Behavior community. There lies Minto Bell (1780-1890), one of Bilali Muhammad's seven daughters. Everyone in the cemetery is buried to the east, a remnant of their Muslim roots. Jojo and I could only look at it through the fence, a recent addition to replace a gate. With the gate, people would come in to take items off gravesites and sketch headstones. What to them was a free-for-all is sacred to descendants. I longed to walk among the mossy oak trees, to read centuries-old headstones and imagine what each person was like. I felt punished for the misdeeds of outsiders who'd been brazen enough to treat the cemetery like their personal playground.

Ironically, Sapelo has never been a playground for the Black people who live there. Maurice says it was never the "nigger heaven" it's often depicted as in historical accounts: "We went from being enslaved, to Howard Coffin (the Hudson Motor Cars tycoon who died on the island in 1937), to Richard Reynolds (the tobacco heir whose widow sold the land to UGA), all these rich people to the state of Georgia, the 'good ol' boys.' We were never free. We had to fight, and we're still fighting."

The fight continues and shifts with the times. A more recent threat to Hog Hummock is climate change. The community inhabits some of the lowest land in Sapelo and could be underwater in the near future if mitigation efforts such as living shorelines don't pan out. It's easy to despair thinking of all the obstacles Sapelonians are up against. How much adversity can one group take? Maurice says he will fight until the end to be able to ride around his community and say "this is" instead of "this was." He jokes about being too stubborn to die, but what happens once he's gone? Plenty of folks want to volunteer for SOLO, but few are open to staying in Sapelo long-term. Who will be left to carry Mrs. Cornelia's torch?

After our tour, Jojo and I gathered our things at the guest house to prepare for our ride to the dock. We wanted to try out a Black-owned restaurant on the mainland in McIntosh called Old School Diner…and to spend the night in a hotel. We needed a bit of relief from the island's bugs and blazing sun before driving home Sunday and getting back to work Monday. Next time we come to Sapelo—and there *will* be a next time—we know to pack insect-repellent clothing, loose, light clothes that cover our skin, and the strongest bug spray we can find. Despite the brevity of our visit, the island earned a special place in both of our hearts. Jojo soaked in its Africanness, which reminded them of their childhood home, Zambia, and ancestral home, Rwanda. I got to bear witness to the good, bad, and ugly of a place that previously existed in my head as a myth. I found Sapelo to be real, raw, imperfect, and beautiful. It reminds me a little of myself.

Before leaving, we sat on the porch with Grace and Adé exchanging last words, phone numbers, and social media handles as Maurice cooked meat on the grill for his supper.

Tongs in hand, Maurice turned to me: "You know you're a Sapelonian, right?"

I thought I misheard him so I asked for clarification.

"Your people are from right across the water."

"Don't tell me that," I laughed. "Now I'm gonna be telling everyone you said that."

I didn't take Maurice's acceptance lightly. We are from two different generations. He is a cisgender heterosexual man, I am a queer, non-binary woman. Yet he stamped me with approval and made me feel like my words about Sapelo matter. I know his standards are too stringent to actually consider me a Sapelonian, but I think he senses my heart is in the right place, even if my rendering of his home doesn't come out exactly how he wants. I felt so pleased by his comment, I momentarily forgot about all the bugs and the sun baking my skin.

When Maurice called me in February 2023 to ask if I knew any reporters who could cover descendants' fight to have input on a statewide bill, HB 273, proposing changes to the Sapelo Island Heritage Authority, it felt good to be able to support from afar. I reached out to colleagues at the online publications *Reckon* and *Prism*, who were both able to cover the story, and a slew of outlets followed their lead. Through media and coalition organizing, including visits to the state capital, Maurice, Josiah "Jazz" Watts, and other descendants got legislators to agree to changing the language of the bill to specify resident members of the board must be descendants.

HB 273 didn't pass, but the energy around their efforts shows the descendants of Sapelo's enslaved Africans are nowhere near done fighting to save their ancestral land. Real change doesn't happen in statehouses.

Mrs. Cornelia's magic persists.

A Rwandese basket and a Gullah Geechee basket sitting side by side on a shelf in Neesha's dining room.

Baskets

I HEARD A LOT OF JOKES IN COLLEGE ABOUT MAJOR-
ing in "underwater basket weaving." The phrase, spat out by right-wing
pundits to ridicule the humanities, is meant to demean disciplines
not linked to a profitable profession and fields founded by anyone
not male and white. I majored in journalism but minored in history
and gravitated toward electives like African American and gender
studies. The humanities helped me think critically and broaden my
worldview beyond my small, rural hometown, where compliance and
conformity had been drilled into my brain by authority figures my
entire life. I grew up being told to "shut up" and "be quiet," and to
always color inside the lines. White classmates got away with being
loud and defiant, while the same behavior landed my Black neurodi-
vergent self in silent lunch. In humanities courses, for the first time

ever, I questioned if and why things had to be this way. If this is what underwater basket weaving feels like, I thought, count me in.

The humanities teach us how to be better humans. That's what the humanities did for me. They gave me a political analysis and lessons on how to resist personal and systemic injustice. And another thing: Underwater basket weaving isn't the insult people think it is. It's actually high praise.

The phrase likely entered the American vernacular via a 1956 magazine article describing how Inuit peoples soak willow reed in water to make it more pliable for basket weaving and was then subverted into an insult that conjures up the bizarre image of a person submerged underwater whilst weaving a basket. Basket weaving doesn't get the respect it deserves due to its association with Indigenous peoples and women, and the impermanence of the materials.

Baskets aren't seen as high art because they break down over time, but to me, their transience makes them even more special. Each detail necessitates close examination simply because it won't last forever. Basket weaving is an ancient practice, an art, a trade, and a science. It's in danger of becoming extinct if we continue devaluing it. There's no such thing as a basket weaving machine, and thus, the craft uniquely affirms the human experience.

Each basket has a story, a life of its own, a maker who learned at the feet of their forebears. Each pattern is intentional and precise. Basket weaving is a sacred dance—an invocation of the ancestors through an intricate finger waltz. Baskets are portals to the past that can teach us as much as any book if we let them.

Baskets can instill in one a sense of pride. I discovered this when, at the invitation of my writer friend and colleague, Aminata Traore-Morris,

I attended a Gullah Geechee forum with my wife, Jojo, in Hinesville-Liberty County, fifty miles north of my hometown. Growing up, I didn't spend much time in Liberty. I mostly drove past it while driving to Savannah, the "big city," to go shopping. But we would visit cousins there every now and then.

After her mother died in childbirth, my great-grandmother—who we called Mother—was raised in Liberty County by relatives in a town called Midway, so named because of its location between the Altamaha and Ogeechee rivers. Mother is who raised my mama for most of her childhood, carting her and her other grandchildren to Midway on Sundays to eat and commune with family members. They picked plums and apples from trees, sending Mama home with preserves. As a child, Mother attended Dorchester Academy, a segregated Black school in Midway opened for freedpeople in 1869 and closed in 1940. Most of the school burned down in the 1930s, but one building remains, once used by the Southern Christian Leadership Conference as an organizing hub during the Civil Rights Movement. I shared this history with Jojo as we drove past the large brick building with white columns. I remembered first seeing the school during a 1994 family reunion, during which I stared at distant cousins through my big, pink bifocals.

As we drove into Hinesville for the forum on a bright Saturday morning in February 2020, I didn't recognize much but everything felt familiar. I rolled down the car window to indulge in the warmth, a welcome reprieve from winter in Atlanta. There were all the modern trademarks of a small coastal Georgia city: Walmart, Zaxby's, Applebee's, Dollar General. Despite corporations stripping away the uniqueness of place, there were reminders of a different way of life. Oak and pine trees lined the virtually empty streets. We arrived at the Liberty County Performing Arts Center, where we walked to the entrance alongside a handful of Black women wearing matching cotton dresses, white aprons, and their hair wrapped in scarves, and a white-bearded Black man wearing a cowboy hat and overalls. One of the ladies smiled as she opened the door for us.

When the program started, I learned who they were: the Gullah Geechee Ring Shouters. I clapped along to their rhythms. Their percussion came courtesy of a washboard, a stick, and their hands, which they clapped as they walked around in a circle while singing and dancing in a ceremony called a ring shout. They sang familiar songs like "Amazing Grace," "Wade in the Water," and "Kumbaya." They informed us kumbaya is Gullah Geechee for "come by here," news to me. It's wild to think this global song originated in the same town where Mama and Grandma were raised. The Shouters sang unfamiliar songs, too, but I heard echoes of home in them. They belted out songs from deep inside their diaphragms, their voices tinged with the same will for survival that reverberated through the walls of my childhood church deep in Geechee country. I felt a sense of belonging.

The forum reintroduced me to what it means to be Gullah Geechee. I didn't know much about the Gullah Geechee as a kid, but I knew enough to see them as "other." The Black folks who identified themselves as such at our school assemblies and on TV talked in funny, Caribbean-sounding accents and dressed like Aunt Jemima. I knew, like me, they descended from enslaved West Africans who called the coast of Georgia and other Southern states "home," but I never associated myself with *those* people who maintained West African traditions. I saw myself as another "regular Black girl" with no ties to my African past.

After the program ended, Jojo and I met a Geechee basket weaver with a crown of long locs, Jennifaye Singleton of Charleston, South Carolina, owner of Geechee Sweetgrass Baskets. Her passion for weaving baskets bloomed in 1990 under the tutelage of her aunt. We *oohed* and *aahed* over her elaborate wares. Baskets of every size and style you could think of. Ones with elephant ears, handles, knots, and loops, others shaped like medallions. Large "rice fanna" baskets traditionally used to separate grain. Laundry baskets, bread baskets, fruit baskets. They sat alongside other items woven with sweetgrass: bracelets, rings, earrings, necklaces, hairbows, dolls, crosses, clocks, wreathes, roses, and ornaments.

Singleton also had Easter baskets for sale, reminding me of how I used to feel so loved receiving a basket specially made for me. I could barely sleep on Easter eve and awoke at the crack of dawn to delight in my pastel loot. Come Easter morning, I knew there would be a basket waiting for me even if we didn't make it to church. Despite Mama's jam packed schedule as a single mother and registered nurse, each year we kids woke up to something beautiful on Resurrection Sunday. The baskets were also for repurposing, too pretty and heart-felt to throw away.

I received my last basket while visiting home my freshman year of college. Upon returning to school, I displayed my basket on a shelf in my cramped dorm room. Once the spring semester ended, I tossed it in the dorm dumpster before driving home—an unwitting goodbye to the comforts and certainties of childhood. My grandma died that summer, and nothing was ever the same. The next Easter, I woke up to no basket in my on-campus apartment. I wasn't a kid anymore. Mama had moved back to the Bronx after two decades away for better job opportunities. I was my own responsibility. Although I'm not a Christian, I'll probably get my child an Easter basket. I want them to feel special like I did.

Jojo and I wanted to buy so many pieces from Singleton but settled on a small bread basket. We had to leave right before she taught a basket weaving class, but I hope another chance arises. I look forward to clumsily weaving my family's story with sweetgrass.

Baskets allow us to traverse seas and land masses. My wife's parents' house in the Corn Belt is filled with baskets from their country of origin, Rwanda. I visited them for the first (and only) time in 2016 for the high school graduation of one of Jojo's brothers. Mr. and Mrs. I picked me and Jojo up from the airport in their van, greeting us with their customary three cheek kisses and a handshake. They drove us to their large suburban home, and we had scarcely put our bags down when Mrs. I asked us, "Ready to get to work?"

My wife had warned me this would happen and about how gendered labor in their culture was. Jojo is rather vocal about not agreeing with it, even to their relatives, but usually adheres to customs when around family—which isn't very often. If I were a man, I would've been exempt from helping prepare for the celebration, but I happily obliged, walking briskly between the kitchen and the deep freezer in the garage to fetch ingredients.

I knew Mrs. I didn't approve of me being married to her daughter and probably never would. I try not to let this bother me. My in-laws' acceptance would be lovely, but it's just not realistic. Some Africans on the continent view queerness as a Western invention, despite the existence of historical queer and gender-variant figures such as Mwanga II (1868-1903) of Buganda, a Bantu kingdom in Uganda, which borders Rwanda. White evangelists from the U.S. are responsible for spreading LGBTQIA+ hate in several African countries, including in Uganda where the president signed a law to make homosexuality punishable by incarceration or death in May 2023. There's also documentation of ancient queer and gender-variant people in the Kingdom of Rwanda. Today, being LGBTQIA+ isn't outlawed in Rwanda, but the community is discriminated against all the same. There are no laws explicitly protecting them nor is gay marriage allowed.

My in-laws are direct products of the society in which they were raised. They never learned how to love a queer person. I have grace for them because they created one of my favorite people in the world. Of course acceptance from Jojo's parents would mean a lot to me. I would love "congratulations" texts and gifts on special occasions like when I graduated with a Master of Fine Arts degree. My parents rarely tell me they're proud of me, so I would gladly welcome praise from my in-laws. But I don't feel like it's my place to disrupt how they feel about queer and trans people. I wouldn't dare tell Mrs. I my true gender lies somewhere on the spectrum between man and woman, if not beyond. I don't see gender nor sexuality as binary. Mrs. I might never be able to understand or accept this.

Although liberal arts taught me to fight to be myself, sometimes life requires compromise. I try to be an idealist while also keeping my feet firmly planted in reality. Both me and Jojo's families were brought up in queerphobic, transphobic versions of Christianity that are difficult—often impossible—to contend with. I choose to dedicate my energy elsewhere rather than exhaust myself trying to change their minds. Sometimes I hide certain aspects of myself around Jojo's family and my own because it makes life less stressful. I love our families even if our politics aren't aligned, and I know they love us, even if they might not always show it. I want to make them comfortable if I'm able. I do this knowing I get to be exactly who I want to be in most other parts of my life.

Jojo is more courageous and outspoken than me; I feel like they show more of their authentic self to our families. I try to seem as "normal" as possible around them. I tone down my wacky, bright outfits, put extra care into my enunciation, squeeze my eyes tight when they bless a meal. I shave my armpits. Despite being queer and American, during my trip to my in-laws' house, I wanted to prove to them, and to myself, I could play the role of a good and obedient African daughter. I wanted them to see me as fundamentally good. Whenever Mrs. I needed a hand, both Jojo and I came running.

Near the end of the trip, our efforts were rewarded.

"Here," Mrs. I said as she reached into a glass cabinet to pull out two baskets for us to take home: one the shape of a shallow bowl with a five-pointed blue and red star, the other palm-sized with a cone-shaped top embroidered with the country name, "RWANDA."

I grinned as I stroked the ridges of our new gifts. These baskets were an extension of my in-laws, carried across an ocean to retain their memories. Baskets remind my wife's parents of their home and its sloping valleys, rolling hills, and pristine lakes. Gifting them to us was a small act of intimacy. A few baskets may not seem like a big deal, but I'm grateful for these tokens of appreciation.

Baskets have the capacity to bring folks together. Basket weaving brought Hutu and Tutsi women together in Rwanda after the country's bloody 1990s conflicts. The widows of dead husbands and mothers of dead sons formed basket weaving cooperatives to sustain themselves, and their wares came to be known as "peace baskets." The baskets from Mrs. I were a kind of peace offering, bridging beliefs, continents, and generations. She didn't respect my sexuality but still wanted me to have something beautiful.

Jojo and I packed our new baskets with care, choosing the perfect places for them when we got home. We've moved a few times since then, and the baskets have accompanied us every mile. I wouldn't dare give them away. Now they live in the office of our home, the bigger one on a shelf, the other on our altar, flanked by beloved photos and art. They breathe life into the room and remind me how finding common ground can mend the ugliest of differences.

Gullah Geechee sweetgrass baskets are distinctly West African. There are two of them in my dining room, and when I look at them I feel less unmoored—like I'm from somewhere special where they make special things.

I grew up hearing from other African Americans we didn't have a culture because we lost it after being stolen from our motherland. My face burned in my eleventh grade U.S. history class when I couldn't answer exactly where my ancestors were from as we went around the room sharing. Sometimes I get jealous when Jojo speaks Kinyarwanda, feeling less than for not knowing my native tongue(s). As a young adult, the humanities allowed me to unpack the lie I was devoid of culture. Influences from enslaved Africans and their descendants permeate all parts of American and global culture—music, media, how we talk, tweet, and dress. Our ways of life are omnipresent. I have no reason to be ashamed of my ancestors' vast societal contributions.

Gullah Geechee sweetgrass baskets are proof African Americans never fully lost our native traditions. Our Gullah Geechee and Rwandan baskets reinforce a shared lineage between me and my wife when it sometimes feels like our families come from different planets. A group of Rwandan and Gullah Geechee women artisans created a pair of baskets in honor of the United Nations' 2021 International Day of Peace, and displayed them in Charleston's airport. The loops of the Gullah Geechee basket are meant to represent connection, while the black and brown women figures holding hands on the Rwandan basket signify solidarity. The artisans plan to continue collaborating.

If it weren't for the humanities, I might not appreciate the value and beauty of baskets, and the labor and history behind them. I might not even see the value and beauty in myself. I grew up conforming to our mainstream, whitewashed society. Rarely did I see myself in the K-12 curriculum; now I know this was by design. Black history, African American studies, and gender studies instructed me not to see myself as inherently inferior. When students study so-called underwater basket weaving, they learn the U.S. is rooted in colonization, land theft, and chattel slavery. My in-laws were first educated in their homeland, and my parents went to underfunded Southern schools, then both sets of parents received degrees in technical professions in the U.S. Despite their advanced education, I believe my parents and in-laws were taught through frameworks that privilege whiteness, maleness, heterosexuality, cisgenderism, and Christianity. This is why our beliefs diverge so greatly. They were taught to suppress what made them "different," while college taught me to accept and celebrate differences. The choice I've made in suppressing myself, temporarily, is one to preserve my own peace around our families. Whether I'll do this forever, I can't say, but for now, this is how we can be together.

The political right has always suppressed and oppressed students from the margins; mainstream media has only just begun to pay attention. As of June 12, 2023, there have been 1,477 instances of book bans this year, according to PEN America. In 2023, the State of Florida rejected an Advanced Placement African American Studies course from being offered in schools, deeming it "woke indoctrination" and "historically inaccurate." People like Florida governor Ron DeSantis hate education in "underwater basket weaving" because it unveils America's ugly truth. Since the powers that be obscure the truth so successfully, people like me are seen as outliers in our families. The burden falls on us to change our families' minds, which are unfortunately often set in stone.

Most Black queer and trans people don't get to indulge in the humanities. I understand why and how I've been tokenized and granted access to certain academic spaces: My skin is between light and medium brown, I "talk properly," and I've been thin most of my life, among other privileges. By no means am I arguing folks need academia to set their minds free. Social media is a powerful tool for introducing people to social justice; although, it's not always credible, and tech CEOs like Elon Musk at X (forever Twitter to me) are deliberately making it harder for us to access this information. Popular education spaces outside of traditional classrooms are also vital in helping people form political identities and beliefs. But such spaces are few and far between, especially in the rural South. It's hard to say whether I would have been exposed to liberatory ideologies if I hadn't attended a university.

In the next world, everyone will be able to access the humanities in both traditional and nontraditional classrooms. We'll all have time and resources to create, theorize, dissect our own hearts, minds, and identities, and find meaning in the everyday. We'll all have time to meditate on baskets and how they signify the ways in which Africans across the globe, despite our real and perceived differences, are bound to each other due to our shared cultural practices—how baskets can bind a person of Geechee descent to a person from Rwanda.

The medium-sized bread basket with elephant ear handles on my dining room shelf reminds me of these ties. Jojo and I bought it during a weekend getaway to Charleston. I wanted to forget about grad school, Jojo wanted to forget about work, and both of us wanted to forget about the pandemic. We walked past a man downtown in a straw hat diligently bundling sweetgrass and pine needle, and coiling it into circles. Now we own a piece of the maker and his lineage forever. Each circle inside of the basket is dwarfed by the next to form one circular vessel. Each circle is a generation birthing the next, building onto an ancient tradition.

II.
Bloody Marshes

Coastal Contradictions

You can almost hear
        a mother weep as her world
                is stolen away.

The face on the side
　　　of the tabby building smiles
　　　　　　in spite of his fate.

Confederate States.
          It is said they dissolved yet
                    their relics endure.

You cannot ignore
            symbols of the New South are
                        replacing the Old.

We cannot unite
        until we look at the truth
                of Black versus White.

DreamDust mural by Cullen Peck in downtown Brunswick, Georgia depicting three children sitting on a wire.

How to Divide a Coastal Georgia Town

1. POUR THE BONES AND FLESH OF THREE HUNDRED eighty-eight thousand West Africans into eighty-two quintillion gallons of saltwater. Bring to a hard boil, turn down to a simmer, cover with a lid.

2. Sprinkle the resulting concoction throughout thirteen colonies in the western hemisphere of the world. Yield fields of rice and sea island cotton by the marshes and waterways of the ancestral home of the Timucua peoples. Name this area after the duchy of Brunswick-Lüneburg in Germany. Stir in ample doses of bondage, domination, hangings, whippings, and rape. Grow this institution like kudzu.

3. Chip away at the kudzu with slave rebellion, abolition, civil war, civil disobedience, and Reconstruction. Resist with disenfranchisement, segregation, and mob violence. Hose down burning crosses and burning homes.

4. Pretend the Confederacy lost and its supporters are dead and gone when Confederate symbols are still alive. Pretend a twenty-foot-tall Italian marble monument of a humble Johnny Reb hasn't stood in a Brunswick, Georgia, public park for one-hundred-twenty years. Bury the reality of the town's four-hundred-eighty-foot-tall bridge named after Sidney Lanier, the Confederate poet.

5. Serve empty promises of equity after three centuries of systemic racism.

6. Spark a fire after a white man murders a Black man in Brunswick for running for exercise, then for his life, through a subdivision a mile and a half from his own front door. Stoke the flames with anger, confusion, and fear. Debate whether the Confederate monument should be removed out of public sight until you've reached gridlock. Marinate in the indecision. Drive a knife into the rift. Let the laceration bleed.

Love is Hope *mural by Kevin Bongang in downtown Brunswick, Georgia depicting the words "Love is Hope" and imagery from coastal Georgia in bright colors.*

The Power of Hate

I take off my glasses to rub sleep out of the inner crevice of my eye. I wish I was in bed instead of digesting a blueberry Pop-Tart in first period. My loud redhead friend, Candi, sits to my left, and Travis, a quiet redheaded boy, sits to my right. Señor Smith leads the class in counting en español. Once, doce, trece, catorce. I stifle a yawn. Despite my persistent sleepiness in Spanish I, I've earned 100s on nearly every test and quiz. My teacher calls me Estrella. Star. I can get away with being half awake.

The classroom door bursts open. The language arts teacher from across the hall walks in with wind in her long, blonde hair. Her face is paler than usual.

"Turn on the TV, Sam," she says breathlessly. "A plane just crashed into the World Trade Center."

MAY 5, 2020

About a month ago, despite not seeing him in fifteen years, I recognized his name immediately in a *New York Times* article: Travis McMichael, the redheaded boy who sat beside me in Spanish class. Outside of that class, our paths never crossed. He was one of the kids who didn't think twice about wearing clothes and driving a pickup truck adorned by the Confederate flag. He was the kind of kid my friends and I steered clear of because we knew he didn't like our kind.

I felt sick to my stomach as I read how Travis shot and killed Ahmaud Arbery, a young Black man who'd been out on a jog. The quiet redneck was now an accused killer. The article featured a photo of a makeshift memorial with a cross, flowers, and balloons near the spot where Ahmaud bled to death. Travis alleged he and his father, Greg McMichael, chased Ahmaud down because he'd previously broken into homes in their neighborhood, Satilla Shores. Of course, he claimed it was self-defense. Standing his ground. The murder happened nearly three months ago, and Travis and his father, who used to work as a cop for the police department that declined to detain him, have yet to be arrested. The case reeks of corruption. I wish it didn't feel so familiar.

Today, one video dominates my Facebook, Twitter, and Instagram feeds. I watch Ahmaud jog as he is blocked in by Travis's and another person's trucks.

※

SEPTEMBER 11, 2001

Señor Smith follows the other teacher's command to turn on the TV. We all look up at it mounted in the top right corner of the room. A second plane just hit the South tower. The screen is filled with smoke and fire. We've never seen anything like this, not even worldly Señor Smith whose mouth is agape. This sort of thing never happens in our America, the "leader of the free world." And New York City feels a world away from us in small town Georgia.

But really, it's remarkably close. Although I have yet to visit, I have relatives in NYC: my oldest sister, all three of my older brothers, two nieces, a great-aunt, a cousin, and lots of family friends. My stomach turns. What are the chances a family member was inside or near the World Trade Center in a city of millions?

We sit silently and watch the tragedy unfold, the flames and billowing smoke, uncertain of everything we've ever been told about our country. Maybe some of us want to cry or scream, but we don't. Maybe because we are teens trying to play it cool, or maybe because we are shell-shocked. It all feels like a movie.

I focus on putting one foot in front of the other—on moving from one classroom to the next. Instruction goes out the window. The TVs are never on in the cafeteria, but they're on today. The TV is on in every one of my classes. Shortly after first period, there are two more plane crashes, one at the Pentagon, another at a Pennsylvania field. I already know my country is not perfect by far. After all, I descend from enslaved Africans. But this is the first time I'm seeing how much the United States is hated elsewhere in the world.

After-school activities are canceled. My usual afternoon at cheer practice is thwarted. Mama is in a somber mood when she picks up me and my sister. Our family members are okay, but there was a close call. Aunt Vee would've been working at her office in the Twin Towers if she hadn't gone to jury duty (turned out, she'd shown up on the wrong day). Why did the Lord spare her and not the others? We go to Grandma's apartment, and I sit right in front of her wooden television set. The attacks are everywhere. The same words are uttered over and over. Al-Qaeda. Osama bin Laden. Saddam Hussein. Taliban. Americans being portrayed as the good guys who did absolutely nothing to provoke a terrorist attack. Talking heads saying reverently, "May God Bless America."

Grandma chuckles about another time of crisis, when Ronald Reagan's Secretary of State told the press he was "in control" in a self-important way after the president was critically shot. Making light of serious situations is our family's coping mechanism. Grandma's laughter indicates perhaps it isn't the end of the world. She chats with Mama while preparing dinner. I feel safe with Grandma because she has survived so much. I try to be brave like her.

MAY 5, 2020

In the video, Travis gets out of his truck, shotgun in hand, as his father stands in the truck bed with a Magnum revolver. A struggle between Travis and Ahmaud ensues. They are out of view when you hear the gun go off once and then twice. Travis proceeds to shoot Ahmaud at point-blank range. He walks away as Ahmaud falls face first to the ground. I turn off autoplay, but I can't go to any corner of the internet or turn to any news station without seeing the video.

Even if I didn't know one of the men who killed him, and even if the area in the footage weren't familiar to me, to watch a man die this way, on repeat, is horrific. I am stuck in the most terrible nightmare.

Again. I've been here before with Trayvon Martin and Michael Brown and Sandra Bland and so many other innocent Black people slaughtered by cops and white supremacists. Some argue sharing these murder scenes can agitate people into action against such inhumane acts, but overexposure is real. These videos become sensationalized. And slowly, I find myself becoming desensitized to bloody, senseless violence against people who look like me.

Yet Ahmaud's murder haunts me. We went to the same schools and knew the same people. We walked the same hallways and streets. I can't shake the video of his last moments on Earth from my head. Sleep won't come easy tonight.

I can't help but think of Emmett Till, a fourteen-year-old Black boy visiting his family in Mississippi who was beaten, shot, and drowned by two white men in 1955 for flirting with a white woman who confessed decades later he never flirted with her. Not that flirting with someone ought to get you killed. One of my old history professors said photos of Emmett's mutilated body helped catalyze the Civil Rights Movement. I wonder if that's something folks say to convince themselves his death was not in vain. I wonder if the video of Arbery's murder will one day, too, be seen as an inflection point. Maybe something positive could come from it being broadcasted around the globe.

Travis and I sat in the same classroom on a day that changed our country forever. I never imagined one of us would become nearly as notorious as those attacks. Did 9/11 bolster Travis's hate for the foreign, the Black, and the brown? Or did he admire the hijackers for waging violence in the name of their beliefs à la the soldiers of his beloved Confederacy?

✳

When I wake up, the U.S. Capitol is already under siege. It's noon, and I'm taking advantage of winter break to sleep in. I roll over to indulge in my customary social media scrolling before starting my day. Chaotic scenes at the Capitol overwhelm my eyes and brain. I had heard rumblings about "Trumpers" who believed voter fraud resulted in Joe Biden's presidential win planning to protest the counting of electoral votes in Congress today. But the images on my feeds depict a full-fledged riot. Masses armed with flags and weapons. Red baseball caps crowding the steps of the building. Angry people, mostly white, wrestling cops to the ground, ramming their bodies into security barriers, and scaling walls with varying degrees of luck.

The sentiment, "If those were a bunch of Black people, they would never get away with this," explodes on Twitter and eventually tumbles out of Biden's mouth.

I walk into the living room to find Jojo swaddled in a blanket on the couch, watching TV. Their youthful countenance appears blissfully unaware, as it should on one of the last days of their vacation from their stressful nonprofit job.

"Have you heard about what's happening at the Capitol?" I ask.

No, they reply, as I grab the remote control and turn to CNN.

The scenes are as intense and disturbing as 9/11, but the perpetrators are homegrown—just like Travis McMichael. At first, my wife and I take turns gasping, cursing, yelling, and gaping as the rioters breach the Capitol doors. Our black cat, Seven, looks on in confusion. A gray-bearded white man sits with his leg kicked up on a desk in Nancy Pelosi's office like he owns the joint. Wearing a fur hat with horns and red, white, and blue face paint, a tattooed, shirtless white man poses for pictures in Mike Pence's seat in the Senate Chamber. Over and over, the news plays a video of a Black police officer waving a baton while being chased up a set of stairs by a mob. His name is Eugene Goodman, and in the clip, he diverts the rioters away from where the Vice President and Senators are. If it weren't for Goodman's quick thinking, the rioters may have achieved their rallying cry: to hang Mike Pence.

It takes hours for the National Guard to be deployed to the Capitol by Pence. Trump waits until 4 p.m. to publicly ask the rioters to go home. Police don't secure the premises until 8 p.m. The newscasters keep declaring, "What we just witnessed is *not* a protest. This is an *insurrection*." Elected officials and political pundits are repeating the term, labeling the rioters as threats to democracy. Despite having been warned of potential violence, the police forces in D.C. failed to adequately prepare.

Now Congress is back in session, and electoral votes will be counted until the wee hours of the morning. Legislators are giving impassioned speeches. This is a soap opera and a reality show. Whenever Jojo comes into the living room from watching shows on their iPad in our bedroom, I exclaim, "This is a day that will live in infamy!" I remember my grandma, the levity she brought into the room as we watched 9/11 unfold.

No arrests have been made yet. One rioter got shot and killed by a cop while attempting to climb into the Speaker's lobby through a broken window. Black and brown service workers are left to clean up broken glass and debris made by the majority-white mob. If things go as expected tonight, Biden will take office in two weeks.

It all feels like a fever dream. I feel like white supremacists are winning, even if Biden takes office as planned. It seems like there will always be another 9/11 in the pipeline. This country keeps breeding and perpetuating hate, unsurprising since it was founded on stolen land and labor.

I get in bed but toss and turn, wondering if I have the stamina to survive such bleakness.

SEPTEMBER 11, 2021

While at a virtual conference this evening, someone asks, Where were you on 9/11?

It's the twentieth anniversary of the attacks, which begat twenty years of war in Southwest Asia, the so-called "war on terror." Some conference attendees said they weren't born yet, but even they feel deeply affected by it.

A few weeks ago, Joe Biden said the war is over, the same thing his predecessor, Barack Obama, said before. But it isn't. There is less American presence in Afghanistan and Iraq, but the U.S. has spent trillions in multiple countries to "end terrorism," efforts resulting in hundreds of thousands of direct, violent civilian deaths and millions of "indirect deaths" worldwide, displacing more than thirty-eight million people, according to a Brown University study. Murdering those people solved nothing. And when people serving in our military for these wars come home, our government does little to take care of them, neglect I've witnessed in my own family. Between 2001 and 2019, nearly thirty-thousand U.S. service members died by suicide. We will never get back the lives lost due to 9/11. The Taliban is back in power, and the rights of Afghan women and girls are more precarious than ever. The government played on our fears to justify an endless war.

On this twentieth anniversary, patriots tell us to "never forget" while 9/11 survivors and first responders are still fighting for free healthcare to remedy illnesses brought on from inhaling inordinate amounts of toxic dust. They're lucky to have made it this long. Immediately after the Twin Towers collapsed, a photographer captured twenty-eight-year-old legal assistant Marcy Borders covered in dust from head to toe. In the photo, Borders stands on a tiled floor, wearing a long sleeve dress and knee high boots, hair combed to the back. Her necklace and hoop earrings glitter despite the white dust covering her brown skin. Borders appears terrified yet elegant. She came to be known as "The Dust Lady." She battled with depression and addiction resulting from trauma and was in massive medical debt when she died of stomach cancer in 2015.

The question—"where were you"—hovering in the air, I think about how 9/11 trauma seems to be insurmountable. Since narrowly avoiding the attacks, my aunt Vee isn't the same. The old Aunt Vee kept her hair done, dressed to the nines, and led the praise dance team at her church. The new Aunt Vee is unable to take care of herself and rarely leaves her apartment. My family will never get the old Aunt Vee back.

Where was I on 9/11? Watching the Twin Towers fall alongside a future domestic terrorist. Two days after the video of Ahmaud being killed went viral, Travis and Greg McMichael were finally arrested, along with an accomplice, Roddie Bryan. The video undoubtedly aided in their arrests. But even if they remain behind bars for life, they will always be victors in their own eyes and in the eyes of their like minded brethren. They accomplished exactly what they set out to do. Ahmaud will never breathe again, while the men who killed him still are. As we get older, we learn the terrible truth: Good does not always defeat evil. Justice is a dish too seldom served. We can fight hate until our faces turn blue but when a racist white man like Travis successfully kills an innocent Black man, hate is inarguably the victor. When capitalist, imperialist, white supremacist interference in Southwest Asia by the U.S. government provokes men to hijack planes, crash them into buildings, and kill themselves and 3,000 others in the process, hate wins yet again.

Americans are indoctrinated to believe innocents had to die to keep our country safe. But I'm nobody's fool. I know the brutal truth: The war on terror is rooted in the hate of anything that doesn't uphold Christian white cishet male supremacy. And January 6 shows that white supremacists are more emboldened now than ever. They're willing to destroy their own country for what they believe in. Some January 6 rioters were arrested and will soon face trial. But it still feels like we never collectively processed or reckoned with everything that went wrong that day. We don't talk about the nearly ten people who died because of that day, including one police officer who died after suffering two strokes and four officers who died by suicide. I don't believe in policing as an institution, but I don't actively wish harm on individual cops. The Right claims to support "Blue Lives Matter," but they sure didn't care about harming police on January 6.

JANUARY 6, 2021

I can't sleep. The images of the day rush through my head again and again. I can't stop thinking about hate, so I try to think of love instead.

I believe the antidote to these acts of hate is love. I believe in Martin Luther King, Jr.'s beloved community. "Love is creative and redemptive. Love builds up and unites; hate tears down and destroys," MLK wrote in a 1957 article. The beloved community is embodied by the racial uprisings of summer 2020 at the the height of the COVID-19 pandemic.

Ahmaud Arbery's murder was one of a trifecta contributing to the U.S. reaching a boiling point then. A month after his death, police in Louisville, Kentucky, fatally shot a twenty-six-year-old Black woman, an ER tech named Breonna Taylor, in the middle of the night as she slept at her boyfriend's house. Fast forward two months, a Black teenager captured the police murder of George Floyd, a forty-six-year-old Black father, on a Minneapolis street with her cell phone. The video of Floyd gasping for breath and crying out for his mother as a white officer drives his knee into the Black man's neck spread like wildfire.

These three stark indignities served as a magnifying glass, showing America who she really is. Protestors filled the streets to oppose this onslaught of racial terrorism. Not just in the U.S. but around the world. Protestors took care of each other, making sure everyone had access to masks, food, and water. Our oppressions felt more connected than ever. Americans marched for Ahmaud, Breonna, and George, for Palestinians killed by Israeli settlers in the Gaza Strip, and for all casualties of murderous regimes. As roads ran crimson with blood, folks rose up and resisted the normalization of state-sanctioned and white supremacist murders being splashed across our screens. People marched in the streets to dismantle hate, scrubbing at stains left by police and state violence.

My M.O. is usually to be on the frontlines, but it felt too risky to be on the ground last summer because of my chronic illnesses. The vaccine hadn't come out yet. I looked on from my couch with respect and appreciation and donated to bail funds. I prayed for the protestors to triumph over hate. On social media, I shared artists' depictions of Ahmaud in happier times and added the #IRunWithMaud frame to my Facebook profile photo. I pored over pictures and videos of hundreds of thousands of activists putting their bodies on the line for Black lives. I consumed art inspired by Black struggle and Black liberation. Kendrick Lamar rapping "we," as in we Black folks, gon' be alright. Nina Simone singing we're going to get what we're owed in due time in "Mississippi Goddam." Posters from Jospehine Baker, Miriam Makeba, and Hugh Masekela performances framed on my living room wall. I resisted images of Black death in favor of renderings of Black life. I visualized a world that is free for all.

I keep thinking about newscasters calling the crowd today "insurrectionists." But were they really? They didn't like the results of an election, so they stormed the Capitol, a historic first. But we've seen terrorists employ violence to get their way countless times. Calling them insurrectionists sounds too much like empowerment. The January 6 rioters exhibited the behavior of entitled, overgrown brats. They deserve to be named as such.

SEPTEMBER 11, 2001

After dinner at Grandma's, we go home. Everyone's nerves are shot, and we're tired.

I get ready for bed as usual. Mama and my siblings do the same.

The news is still replaying the plane crashes, but I refuse to watch them on my bedroom TV.

I choose sleep instead. I've seen enough.

Matt and the author dressed as Saturday Night Live's Spartan Cheerleaders for their high school's Twin Day, 2004.

The Confederate's Son

ME: A LANKY BLACK GIRL WITH BANGS AND SKIN the color of red brick.

Him: a chubby white boy with olive skin and dark brown hair spiked up with gel.

You wouldn't expect me and Matt to become close friends at our coastal Georgia middle school where kids mostly stuck with their own race. Yet, we clicked instantly after crossing paths at a drama club meeting in seventh grade. Matt had just transferred from the local Catholic school, but his gregarious personality allowed him to avoid adjustment woes that came with being "the new kid."

Matt clogged in the same troupe as our drama club advisor, Mrs. Johnson, and I'd taken tap lessons for years, so we shared a love for hoofing. He taught me clogging routines in Mrs. Johnson's classroom after-school. Since clogging is an unconventional hobby for hetero-sexual males and because Matt rarely hung out with other boys, there were whispers about him being gay. This rumor didn't stop butterflies from fluttering around my stomach whenever he was around. He was one of the first boys who ever hugged me, and I looked forward to his embrace before we boarded our respective buses at the end of the school day.

One of my girlfriends confessed to me she liked Matt, but my crush on him remained a secret. What if he found out, and it ruined our friendship? What if Mama disapproved of his whiteness? My older sisters had never brought a white boy home, and Mama hemmed and hawed when I merely asked to visit white friends' houses. I settled for being Matt's number one fan. I tried to impress him with my burgeoning clogging skills. I cheered him on when he clogged to Backstreet Boys in our school talent show. At a Valentine's Day dance, someone asked if we were each other's date. I swiftly responded, "No," despite desperately wishing the opposite.

I didn't discover Matt's Confederate ties until our junior year of high school. We lost touch in tenth grade when I let my boyfriend, Steven, consume my entire life. I neglected my friends for an entire year, even when Steven tried to control me and called me "stupid" on the regular. Steven belittled me when I didn't act how he expected me to act or do what he expected me to do. One time at the mall, a few feet away from the carousel of my youth, he pinned me to the wall in frustration. I think his anger stemmed from getting picked on as one of the only Asians at school. His sister seemed angry, too, and threatened to beat me up. We broke things off with each other as I wrapped up sophomore year. Things never really got violent. Or at least that's what I told myself since he hadn't left any physical marks. I walked into eleventh grade an independent woman. Matt and I were in the same homeroom and almost all of the same classes. We picked up right where we left off.

After school, we'd catch a ride to Matt's house, where we ate snacks, watched movies, and sang and danced to his favorite musician, Selena, the slain Tejana superstar. As soon as we pulled into his driveway, we were greeted by the Confederate flag flying from a tree in the front yard and on the license plate of his dad's truck alongside a "Heritage, Not Hate" bumper sticker. His dad had dedicated the back room of their modest home to the Old South: A quote from *Gone with the Wind* graced the wall, and Confederate uniforms for Civil War reenactments hung in the closet. Each April for Confederate Memorial Day, Mr. Nelson proudly donned one of his uniforms at the twenty-foot-tall white stone monument downtown bearing the inscription, "In honor of the Confederate soldiers who died to repel unconstitutional invasion…"

The "stars and bars" were part of Georgia's state flag from 1956 until 2001, the year I entered ninth grade—so ubiquitous it barely registered in my consciousness. I didn't consider what the blue "X" and thirteen white stars meant until Confederate flag T-shirts from the Dixie Outfitters store in the mall became popular at my middle school. Piecing together anecdotes from social studies, the History Channel, classmates, and relatives, I realized white folks who believed themselves superior to Black folks worshiped this symbol—folks who claimed to be preserving the history of their ancestors who fought for "the Lost Cause" but omitted the lost cause was slavery. I grew to hate that flag because I hated hate. In PE class, I was usually the last person picked by team captains, regardless of their race, thanks to my crossed eyes, speech impediment, and general awkwardness. How I looked and sounded got me pegged as one of the least desirable girls at school. My chest stung when I witnessed cruelty because

I experienced it so often myself. My heart wrenched at the mere thought of someone being treated badly for things out of their control, including skin color.

In eighth grade, while sitting at a lunch table with Matt and our drama club crew—my only friends—I spotted a white boy across the room wearing the most upsetting shirt I'd ever seen. Emblazoned with the Confederate flag, it read, "These Colors Don't Run," and depicted Black people picking cotton. A switch turned on inside of me. Before I knew it, my gawky limbs were marching across the cafeteria toward him.

I tapped him on the shoulder. "Why are you wearing this shirt?"

I had gotten all fired up to tell him how offensive his shirt was to me and other Black students whose ancestors were enslaved, that he should never wear it to school again. But my admonishment got thwarted by the white woman teacher who appeared by my side.

"I'll talk to him," she said, then ushered the boy toward a cafeteria exit.

I swaggered back to my lunch table with pride. I hadn't had enough time to condemn his shirt outright, but my question implied my opposition. I could've sat there and said nothing like everyone else. I never found out what the teacher said to the boy or if she made him change his shirt, but it didn't matter. None of my friends cheered me on, but it didn't matter. I was a burgeoning voice for the righteous.

Still, I never confronted Matt about his dad's allegiance to the Confederacy. Mr. Nelson never said anything racist around me and barely ever talked. Boisterous Matt seemed nothing like his soft-spoken dad. Matt obsessed over Latin American cultures and talked up his Italian and Portuguese ancestry. We made fun of his dad's addiction to the Old South and classmates who celebrated being Southern and white: their thick country accents, hunting jackets, Dixie Outfitters shirts, and trucks with huge tires. They entertained us so much we decided to dress up as them for Twin Day 2003. We bought matching camouflage shirts and atrocious black mullet wigs at Walmart. The morning of Twin Day, my grandma, who had never formally met Matt, drove me to his house. When I arrived at his front door, he cackled at my appearance then led me to the back room.

"Here," Matt said, pulling out a roll of Confederate flag stickers from a drawer. He stuck one on to the front of his shirt and one on mine.

I didn't think twice about wearing the sticker to school. It was a parody after all—a derivative of the sense of humor we'd adopted from *Mad TV* and *Saturday Night Live*. Matt's mom drove us to school. My "twin" wasn't in first period with me, but I sat right behind him in our second period class, advanced U.S. history. During class, Janet, a Black former homecoming princess who could trace her ancestry back to Sierra Leone, locked eyes with me. She pointed at the front of her shirt where my sticker was, shook her head, and mouthed, "No." Face burning, I ripped the sticker off and prayed nobody else had noticed it, especially not my Black classmates.

My burning cheeks didn't stop me from posing for a picture with Matt later that day. Both of us grinned widely as I draped my arm around him still wearing his sticker. The photo is preserved for time immemorial in our eleventh-grade yearbook. "Love can make you do crazy things," indeed. I loved how Matt accepted me when so many others didn't. I loved going to mass with him, despite being raised Baptist. I loved when he showed me off to his church youth group. I loved going to the beach with him, even though I couldn't swim. I loved renting DVDs at Blockbuster with him on weekends. I loved watching *Friends* together, one of Matt's favorite shows, although I never liked it; I just wanted to be near him. I loved watching *America's Next Top Model* together, a mutual favorite. I loved choreographing dances and acting in school plays together. I loved grinding on each other at school dances. I loved exchanging silly notes with him during class and making up nicknames for our classmates. I loved underage drinking with him. I loved cuddling on his living room couch. I loved staying on the phone with each other all night long. I loved how much I smiled in his presence. When I look at the photo of us in the yearbook, I remember all of that, and I cringe.

I remember the night Matt told me I was pretty as Halle Berry over the phone and sounded like he meant it. I remember the night we sat in the backseat of a friend's truck and nearly cried about potentially being separated for college, "What are we going to do without each other?" I remember when Matt dared me to call a local radio station and dedicate a song to him, which I did: "Dreaming of You" by Selena. I remember when his mom bought me a body pillow for Christmas because I was always laying on his. I remember going to a birthday dinner for one of his family members at Golden Corral, and his paternal grandmother asking if I was his date. I smiled and shook my head; although, I wished I could nod instead. I remember how happy he was when I learned the lyrics to Selena's "Amor Prohibido" for him on a whim. The title in English means, "Forbidden Love."

Also, I remember Matt telling me his deceased maternal grandfather didn't believe in interracial relationships—how it felt like a kick to my gut. He said it not to condemn his grandfather but as a matter of fact. And I remember the time we visited the house of a friend, a white girl, while she babysat a little Black girl, and him saying to me with a snicker about the little girl, "She doesn't like you because you're a nigger."

I had heard him say "nigga" before while rapping and singing and a few other times, when I would raise an eyebrow, and he would look at me defiantly and say, "What? I can say that word." But this was my first time hearing him say the word with the hard "r" *and* directing it toward me. I rolled my eyes in response and mumbled, "Whatever." I thought it was a stupid and random thing to say, yet Matt's words held so much weight to me that I took to them heart, like maybe he was right in some weird way. Despite Matt's racist comments, I didn't want to believe he was racist. My love for Matt functioned like a veil, obscuring what I didn't want to accept. I tolerated it for the longest and even participated. I laughed when he nicknamed younger kids on our Model United Nations team "Hillary Jew" and "Little Black Kid." I never challenged him. Although we didn't end up at the same college, we remained friends after high school. But by the time of our ten-year high school reunion, I was ignoring his phone calls.

We never had a big falling out. Rather, I had a big awakening. I got my first taste of feminism and activism in college, catapulting me into the Occupy movement and then the Movement for Black Lives. The latter movement taught me even the most well-intentioned white people enact and benefit from racism. It is a systemic consequence of history, not just individual, isolated acts. Matt's power and privilege prevented him from seeing the wrongness in putting a Confederate flag on a Black girl's body, his grandfather's thoughts on interracial relationships, and calling me a nigger. The more I learned about white supremacy and racial injustices, the more impossibly ignorant Matt seemed. He had no interest in marching alongside me in the name of Trayvon Martin nor other Black victims of police terrorism. We gradually slipped into different worlds, and he no longer fit into mine. I found new people to love who loved me back and would never call me a nigger. I could've attempted to teach away his racism, but that felt unfair and too great of a burden. Walking away from Matt felt as liberating as being freed from Steven's ridicule. The Confederacy may not have won the war, but it triumphed in ending our friendship.

I unfriended Matt on Facebook in my late twenties, but he still messages every now and then, usually clips from movies we used to laugh at. I rarely message back. If I do, I keep it brief. I changed my phone number, but he calls via Facebook from time to time. I must admit, I'm always curious about why he's calling after all these years, yet I never answer. I can't rekindle our friendship when I'm still trying to figure out who I was back then and why I let him put that sticker on me when just a few years before, I had stomped across the cafeteria to ask a stranger why he was wearing an offensive Confederate T-shirt. Aside from my love for Matt, what made me feel comfortable spending countless hours at his house surrounded by altars to the Confederacy? Why did I compartmentalize or brush off the racist comments he made? If I'm going in the past, it's not for him but instead to interrogate my own actions.

I'm not going to lie: It's fun to look back at our memories from time to time, like the picture of us on Twin Day our senior year dressed as the Spartan cheerleaders from our beloved *Saturday Night Live*, jumping into the sky. We wore big smiles as Matt's mom snapped a photo of us in their front yard leaping while sporting black, red, and white uniforms we made ourselves. The image encapsulates the creativity and fun in our friendship—what initially bonded us together. I mourn the good parts of our relationship and accept the rest as a lesson.

Black Futures Matter / End Citizens Arrest mural by Roderrick Davis in Brusnswick, Georgia depicting a young Black boy wearing a mask, extending his right fist in the air.

Running on King Cotton Row

KING COTTON ROW. PLANTATION CIRCLE. I NEVER thought twice about these street names in my childhood neighborhood until my Aunt Annie visited us from Atlanta the year the city hosted the Summer Olympics. My grandmother's next to youngest sister, Aunt Annie was a bit of a black sheep. She passed of a heart attack when I was nine. She was only forty-eight. While helping my mother move into a new apartment a few years ago, I found a Christmas card from my aunt where she signed off as a "community organizer." I thought *I* was my family's first community organizer. No wonder Aunt Annie sounded so agitated whenever we drove past the "King Cotton Row" street sign. "White people sure won't let go of the past," she would say while sucking her teeth.

1. Shayne Lee

During my first summer home from college, I would go jogging in the evening when the hot sun granted a reprieve. MP3 player blaring in my ears, I was fairly oblivious to my surroundings. The neighborhood was quiet, and most people were inside of their homes. It never occurred to me I was a Black girl running in a mostly white subdivision, one not terribly different from Satilla Shores fourteen miles away where Ahmaud Arbery took his last run. If my skin were darker, if I were a man, my jogs might've concluded with my corpse sprawled across asphalt like Ahmaud's did. *Those three white men spotted Ahmaud, and fear flashed before their eyes.* To them, he represented the annihilation of the white race and the proliferation of babies mixed with Black and white. To them, killing Ahmaud wasn't personal—it was about preservation.

2. Walter Runciman

If I still lived in Brunswick, Georgia, I wouldn't be comfortable running in a majority-white neighborhood like I used to. The murder of Ahmaud shows being Black while running outside in my hometown is a potential death sentence. We always knew we weren't safe, but what happened to Ahmaud gave us proof. *Although Black people are the majority in Brunswick, they don't feel safe, while white people do. They've always wanted safety and are now demanding it in the streets. All they want is what white people already have. Is it not unreasonable for them to be denied protection when the murder of Ahmaud showed the whole world their lives are at stake?*

3. Jeff Greenberg et al.

The mere thought of the Confederate monument being removed from Hanover Square in downtown Brunswick terrifies some people. That slab of marble is the physical manifestation of their ancestors' service to the "Lost Cause." It gives them something to believe in. "Heritage, not hate," they say when challenged about displaying symbols of the Old South. *To manage the terror of their beliefs possibly becoming extinct, these people cling to their Confederate signifiers. They view the Black Lives Matter graffiti on the Confederate monument as an assault on their way of life.*

Notes:

1. John Blake, "There's one epidemic we may never find a vaccine for: fear of black men in public spaces," CNN, accessed May 27, 2020, https://www.cnn.com/2020/05/26/us/fear-black-men-blake/index.html. Historically, Black men have been viewed as a threat, particularly by white people who project their own criminality and hypersexuality onto them. Sociology professor Dr. Shayne Lee calls this phenomenon the "fearful gaze."

2. Robert Longley, "All About Relative Depravation and Depravation Theory," ThoughtCo., accessed August 3, 2021, https://www.thoughtco.com/relative-deprivation-theory-4177591. The late British sociologist Walter Runciman was one of the first scholars to define relative deprivation theory: when a person or group doesn't have something considered essential in their society, knows other people who have the thing, wants to have the thing, and believes they have a reasonable chance of getting the thing. Relative deprivation may compel people to organize collectively for social change.

3. "Terror Management Theory," Psychology Today, accessed February 27, 2022, https://www.psychologytoday.com/us/basics/terror-management-theory. Terror management theory, developed by social psychologists Jeff Greenberg, Sheldon Solomon, and Tom Pyszczynski, describes a concept in which a cultural group manages their fear of death by preserving cultural symbols and ideas that reinforce their superiority over other cultural groups.

III.
Religion & Resistance

Grandma sitting beside Mother while holding Neesha in her lap at an outdoor party.
Late 1980s.

Reproduction

GREENERY ABOUNDS. A STRING OF BALLOONS OVER-
head—some are deflated. Yellow. Blue. Orange. Green. Red. Here sits
three branches of the same tree, three shades of smooth brown skin.
Her reflection is her reflection is her reflection. A moment etched
into time.

I.

The blue-black lady in mid-conversation is the matriarch of the
family, yet she never even knew her own mother. Maybe that's why
she ended up so ornery. Smacks her grands and great-grands' bot-
toms with a switch. But she keeps up a pristine image in her coastal
Georgia hamlet. Business owner, hairdresser, chef, Sunday School
teacher. Five daughters and one stillborn son.

II.

The acorn-complected woman holding the baby is "cosmopolitan country." Smokes a pack of Virginia Slims a day. Fills apartment with furniture from rich white people's homes she works in. Employs her feminine wiles when necessary. Grows sativa in her living room. Fries catfish every Friday eve. James Brown—who she once saw in concert on Jekyll Island—croons on her record player. Two children, a boy and a girl, but her womb is now gone; a man beat it out of her.

III.

The smiling bright-skinned baby with the big forehead and two bottom teeth was a surprise. In the arms of Grandma, Grandma's mama to their left. Product of breakups, makeups, and her father's cocaine sweats. Christened in a white lace gown sewn by her great-aunt, also named her godmother. A chance to absolve familial sins, break generational curses. Third girl in a row. Twenty-seven years later, she wears white when she weds a chestnut-colored woman dressed in yellow, christening gown carefully packed away for the next in line.

IV.

The great-grandma, Mother, taught the baby to follow the rules. To live and die by Baptist teachings. The baby opted to be more like Grandma when she got older. To be free, to experiment. Took birth control to avoid becoming a teen mother, a "family curse." Had sex with boys but dreamed of a girl's lips—although Jesus didn't approve. First generation to attend a four-year college—where Black feminism became her religion. Still sees Grandma and Mother in her reflection. They are the same yet different.

Dunbar Creek, a site in St. Simons Island, Georgia where a group of Igbo people drowned themselves to evade enslavement in 1803.

Trouble the Water

SINK

When I'm seeking courage, I imagine a fictional heroine in a real event. I call her Nneka.

Sulfur invades Nneka's nostrils as she feels the ship come to a halt, waking her up. The thirty-year-old woman sleepily takes in her surroundings, slapping away hordes of gnats. Giant oak trees dripping with moss lie beyond miles of golden marshes. The vast Niger River of her homeland dwarfs this creek. She had tried to brand scenes of home into her brain but after six weeks in shackles under the deck of one ship and then another with only gruel to eat, the images are beginning to fade.

Familiar and strange tongues swirl about Nneka, hotly debating their next move. They are different, but they are kin: seventy-five

Igbo peoples. Upon leaving the bustling port city where they'd been auctioned off on a block, they swiftly devised and executed a plan to commandeer the ship. Ending up on the shores of a creek, the passengers contemplated settling there and starting a new life...until spying an imposing pale figure in the distance.

Terror grips at Nneka's throat. An old lady with cloudy eyes from her village preaches nearby about Chukwu, shouting he will guide them to freedom. Nneka had always enraged her mother when she questioned Chukwu's existence, yet she doesn't know who or what else to believe in as the sun unforgivingly beats down on her skin. Chukwu is everywhere, her mother had always told her. He created the sun. He created the water. He is the sun. He is the water. Chukwu is all-knowing and all-powerful. Surely he will protect them as long as they keep faith. The old lady's words rouse her until she wants to cry but can't because of dehydration. We are warriors, the old lady shouts. We will not bow to these evil white men. We must take to the water if we want to go home. We were not built to be slaves.

Nneka curls into a ball, rocking as she listens to the sermon. Until now, she's never been afraid of the water—in her village, the river is a center of life, sustenance, and ceremony. She flinches at the memory of cat-o'-nine-tails stinging her back at the auction. She knows she will never see her family again. Not on Earth anyway. When the prophetess asks who will walk into the creek, Nneka is in the number. The two women are joined by eleven others.

The group stands in the wet grass beside the water and clasps hands. Nneka tries not to shake as the old lady leads them in prayer. They chant together: The water spirit brought us, the water spirit will take us home. Don't be afraid, the old lady yells. We are headed back home, she points to the ground. Nneka marches with her head high and heart beating out of her chest as water engulfs her lungs.

The onlookers never forget this sight for as long as they live. Later enslaved on the rice and cotton plantations where their ship came ashore, St. Simons Island, Georgia, they are whipped when they dare utter Chukwu's name.

ANOINT

A cluster of Black women dressed in all-white walk into a large tan church with rainbow-colored stained-glass windows and a tall white steeple across the river from St. Simons. They have a special delivery: an infant wearing a white gown and bonnet adorned with lace. The baby girl is held by a tall, light brown-skinned lady with yellow undertones named Nettie with thick hair pulled back to reveal round turquoise earrings. She stayed up all night at her sewing machine to finish the baby's outfit. She wants this day to be perfect. A few months ago, her niece, Sue, moved back to coastal Georgia from New York City to leave a doomed marriage, just in time to give birth to her third daughter. She needs her community to rally around her. Fortunately, she hails from a matriarchy of strong-willed women.

Aunt Nettie plans a christening for the new baby at the family's church in downtown Brunswick—a Black Baptist church founded less than a decade after the emancipation of enslaved Africans. No matter what drama is unfolding among the family, the Church resides at the core of their lives. Prayer can fix anything. Sue appoints Aunt Nettie the baby's godmother. The two women stand side by side at the altar as the pastor sprinkles water on the fidgety baby girl during the last days of summer. The red pews are filled with family and friends, some holding disposable cameras invented just last year: 1986. Aunt Nettie dutifully promises to assist Sue in raising the baby up in the Christian faith. Of course, the baby, who is me, has no say in the matter.

Over the years, we tapered off into the kind of family who only shows up to church on holy days. Mama rested on Sundays since she ran around all week, working one-and-a-half nursing jobs, shuttling four kids to and from extracurricular activities, and cooking dinner five times a week with help from Grandma, who worked one-and-a-half jobs herself. Sometimes I read our big, colorful children's Bible for fun. I interpreted its tales of talking serpents and parting seas as fiction—alternative realms like Stoneybrook, Connecticut, in *The Baby-Sitters Club*.

We started going to church more when I was about nine. I don't remember exactly why we began attending church again; yet, I always associate it with my budding pubescence. I was five feet two inches of out of whack hormones and more than filled out my training bra. I detected shock in Mama's voice when she spotted splotches of blood in my underwear that year. By that time, my family had gone back to an earlier church home on the north end of McIntosh County where Mama and Grandma grew up. I buried my nose in a book as gospel played on the radio during our thirty-minute Sunday morning drives to our white cinderblock church with burgundy trim around the windows in the middle of nowhere. Sunday school at 9 a.m., worship service at 10 a.m., and church finally let out around 2 p.m., when we went down the street to my great-aunt's house to fill our bellies with golden fried chicken, collard greens, rice, mac and cheese, and a buffet of homemade pies and cakes in glass cake stands.

One day, Mama decided to officially rejoin the church during altar call, which happened at the end of each service. She reached for my hand only—not my older sister's or little brother's—and we walked to the front of the sanctuary. I clenched my jaw as the pastor held the mic in front of Mama, his other arm resting on her shoulder. I know Jesus loves me, she said as she patted my hands. I don't remember consenting to being baptized, but somehow we started planning for it. I assumed it came along with being a full-fledged, communion-taking church member, which made me feel grown-up. Since my older sisters had been baptized, it felt like a rite of passage in our family. The morning of my baptism, Mama helped me get dressed in a white headwrap and robe. I sat in the middle front pew during worship service with the other person getting baptized, a man with a Jheri curl who took laps around the church when enraptured with the Spirit. During a prayer, I held hands with a boy sitting in the pew behind me who loudly whispered to his friend, "Her hand feels good." His words made something in my abdomen quicken. This was the impulse Mama sought to wash away.

Toward the end of the service, the organist banged his keys as the church members warbled: "Take me to the waterrr, take me to the waterrr, take me to the waaater to be baptiiized." The pastor guided me to the baptismal pool behind the altar and gestured for me to cross my hands over my chest. I scrunched my eyes up as he dunked me into the water. After, I changed into a frilly white dress to eat fried chicken in the church annex. I reveled in attention that day, but I didn't get the hype. I thought, Now what happens? Because I feel the same as before.

PLAY

Out of boredom, I tagged a textbook with my name during a sixth-grade science class. Later in the semester, a friend used said textbook. She tapped me on the shoulder and pointed to where one of our classmates had written "not cool" and "unpopular" by my name. I've never been knocked down as many times as in sixth grade. I was skinny as a rail except for my protruding breasts, closing in on my adult height of five feet, eight and a half inches. I wore bangs to disguise my large forehead. Chemical relaxers had burned away the hair on the back of my scalp. I begged to get braces to be like the popular kids (Mama consented because she didn't know that was my reason).

I wore the same Mudd and Zana Di flared jeans that graced the pages of my teenage fashion magazines. I wanted to look trendy. I wanted to be cool but was far from it. Peers teased me over my speech impediment and crooked eyeballs. Teachers pulled me out of class to reprimand me for laughing too loudly, muttering underneath my breath, and making sarcastic jokes. My breasts wouldn't stop growing, and my period brought sharp cramps that caused me to double over in pain. My body disgusted me, except for when I snuck moments of pleasure, like watching scrambled soft-core porn late at night on cable channels or binging on a bag of Twizzlers.

A small group of white and white-passing neighborhood girls embraced me during that time—I think because they were outcasts, too, but to a lesser degree: One had anorexia, another had darker coloring due to having Native American ancestry, and a few of them were slightly overweight. These characteristics excluded them from the popular crowd. That's just how things were in middle school circa 1999. Being different wasn't cool. It must've been a weekend or summer when Ashley called my family's landline to invite me to one of their houses. I didn't call Mama at work for permission since I would be only a few streets over. I told my older sister where I was headed. I didn't know where Kristi lived, so Ashley, with her rosy, chubby cheeks and blonde pigtails, met me halfway on her bike. Kristi's three-level house sat on the marsh with a pool on the side, courtesy of her rich stepdad. Swimming was the activity of the day. Not only did I not know how to swim, but I had just gotten my hair relaxed at a salon and dipping into chlorinated water would surely ruin the expensive treatment.

With trepidation in my heart, I piled into Kristi's mom's van with the other girls and went to Walmart, where they picked out floats, beach balls, and other water accessories. I kept looking over my shoulder, hoping no one who knew Mama saw me with a bunch of white girls and one of their moms, who always wore her skirts short. I might get a belt to the hand if Mama found out I left the house without her permission to hang out with white people she didn't know; she didn't trust white people, especially not random ones—she trusted Black people whose families she knew. Back at Kristi's house, the other girls changed into their bathing suits and jumped into the pool. I sat off to the side as they shrieked with laughter playing volleyball and Marco Polo. Even among friends, I was the outsider.

I was growing tired of all the restrictions forced upon me. I couldn't get in the pool because of my relaxed hair. I couldn't date white boys because of my race. I couldn't have sex until marriage because of my religion. I felt too young to have sex then, even though a few of my classmates were already doing it. But I saw nothing wrong with having sex once I was in high school, no matter what the Bible said. I couldn't do anything fun because, because, because. I was beginning to understand why Eve bit into that apple.

SOAK

The year before Donald Trump got elected, I traveled to the Olympic Peninsula with my spouse, Jojo, and three friends for a two-mile hike to natural hot springs. Early in the morning, we drove north of Seattle, where we all lived, to take a ferry ride across the Puget Sound. I had never seen a ferry of this magnitude and marveled at being able to drive onto it. We walked upstairs to enter the ferry, where riders relaxed in booths and bought refreshments. We posed for a photo beside a large 3D map of the peninsula.

Wind nipped at our faces when we went out on the deck and said "goodbye" to the city skyline and "hello" to mountains and rainforests and orcas leaping out of the clear blue water. I was used to being surrounded by waterways, but back home they were more green than blue and were hugged by swamps and marshes instead of a rolling landscape. We were all in good spirits except for Maria, who'd just broken up with her boyfriend of a few years. I thought she was better off without him—he identified as a "meninist," for God's sake—but I tried to muster up empathy. A hobbyist photographer, she wandered alone around the deck, snapping pictures with her professional camera.

It took about thirty minutes to arrive at our destination, the port of a small community in Kitsap County. Hyperconscious of our Black and brown bodies in a white space, we brunched at a cute, rustic spot, then resumed our journey. We drove two hours northwest to get to Olympic Hot Springs, sharing cannabis edibles and discussing the state of the world as we passed farms and villages that hearkened to the possibility of a simpler way. White supremacists were beginning to slither out of their caves, and their power dynamics were trickling into *our* communities. Most of us were part of a collective of young queer and trans community organizers of color, and movement elders were becoming our biggest critics. They told us our collective wouldn't last because similar ones had dissolved quickly in the past. They acted as if there were a quota for how many Black and brown-led social justice groups could exist in Seattle. "It's like we're all fighting for scraps," I remarked. "Can't we all just get along?"

The expansiveness surrounding us made our problems feel small. Jojo maneuvered our Kia Sorento uphill to get to the trailhead. We parked, got out of the car, and were greeted by a green, brown, and orange kaleidoscope of trees: cedar, spruce, evergreen, fir, and maple. We set off marching to our destination, equipped with backpacks, water bottles, and snacks. On the way up, we read a flier with an old white man's picture nailed to a tree. He'd gone missing on the trail. "Oh my God," I squawked. "Stick together, y'all." At one point, Maria stopped in her tracks. "I'm fine," she said. She continued to lag behind. We crossed a long foot bridge and a long tree bridge with rushing streams below.

We saw steam rising as we approached the hot springs, each one circled by barriers of rocks. Everyone but Maria peeled off most of our clothing and plopped into the first hot spring we came across. We weren't bound to anyone's rules but our own. The water was murky with bacteria, but I felt alive—nearly naked in fifty-degree weather in the middle of a rainforest. I admired my spouse and friends' breasts and tattoos, peered over at Maria leaning against a tree and journaling in a notebook. I'd never imagined this would be my life: soaking on top of the world, thousands of miles away from home. This was belonging. My new religion of not giving a fuck. I'd washed my hands of Christianity when family members used the Bible to condemn me for coming out as queer in my early twenties. I evacuated the faith of Aunt Nettie and Mama. I made the decision to be my own god.

FLOAT

I've always hidden that I can't swim. I intentionally avoid the topic. I lived close to the beach as a child, but Mama didn't prioritize swim lessons for us kids, and we didn't live close to public pools. Lots of my friends in high school were lifeguards, and they laughed at my lack of water skills. I never asked them to teach me. When I'm back home by the Atlantic, I can't shake the thought of a slave ship on the horizon of the ocean. I was born minutes away from where the Igbo peoples drowned themselves and Jekyll Island, where one of the last slave ships illegally landed. My home is a place where slavery haunts the water. When I look at the ocean, fear washes over me as if I were my ancestors about to be whisked across the ocean in a slave ship, away from everything I know to a life of sheer hell.

My spouse didn't laugh when I told them I couldn't swim. "I can only doggy paddle," they shrugged. They lost teeth in a childhood diving accident in Zambia, and that's when their swim education ended. Swim lessons were something we could share. We signed up for Saturday morning classes at our local YMCA and purchased swimsuits on sale. Mine was a sporty but funky one-piece with bursts of color and black and white stripes on the straps. I liked how I looked in it. I looked like the real thing.

I struggled to wake up on the first day of class. When the cold air outside hit my face, I yearned for my bed. Jojo and I got changed in the locker room, then met our instructor at the pool, Steve, a Black guy who appeared to be in his early twenties. We were joined by two classmates: a man starting from scratch and a lady looking to improve her skills. The first skill we needed to master was floating on our backs. Jojo made it look easy. When my turn came, I felt my legs resisting. Use your core, Steve advised. Focus. He said my muscular body type made me less buoyant. I think he was trying to make me feel better. Water flooded my ears each time I leaned back into the pool, poking my pelvis out as far as possible.

I imagined Nneka, submerging. Could she swim?

I pretended the muted voices above the water were my ancestors, nudging me to float on.

Grandma, a daughter of "cursed" McIntosh County, Georgia, posing by one of her many plants.

The Curse

LET MAMA TELL IT, HER HOMETOWN IS CURSED.
She first told me and Jojo the story during a visit to our Atlanta home
in 2019. While sitting on a yellow Ikea chair in our living room, iPad
in hand, she told us Darien, Georgia, was cursed by the mother of a
Black man lynched there years ago. She didn't know the mother nor
son's name but knew some of the family's relatives. She grew up hearing her grandmother talk about the curse.

The curse, Mama explained, is why Darien struggles so much.

"That's why nothing succeeds there, not the outlet mall, not the
juvenile detention center, nothing," Mama said matter-of-factly.

I don't remember what moved her to mention this, but I've been
obsessed with finding out more ever since. I have friends and acquain-
tances who've heard of the curse, but nobody knows the details.

They heard it from their elders. Some say only the city of Darien is cursed, others say it's the whole county. I found a post on Roots to Glory Tours' Facebook page about how the curse led to the downfall of McIntosh County's cotton, rice, lumber, and commercial fishing industries: "As the story goes, there was a lynching of a young man in the main town. His mother is reported to have put a curse on Darien that the city would no longer be successful. According to the locals, the curse worked." However, it doesn't say from whom exactly the curse originated. And I haven't been able to get a solid origin story on this folklore from elders.

One day, I hope to confirm whether the curse is linked to two consecutive lynchings that I've researched. On September 8, 1930, two Black men, George Grant and William "Bubber" Bryan, were lynched by a white mob in Darien after being accused of trying to rob a bank and then allegedly killing the police chief, Robert L. Freeman, and wounding a bank guard and two other white men, a deputy and a state employee. A governor-appointed state militia tried and failed to stop the townspeople from taking "justice" in their own hands. After a white mob of hundreds killed Bryan, Darien's mayor put out a statement that it had been a case of mistaken identity; they had actually been looking for Bryan's brother. Then, a rumor spread that the deputy had also died, a false report from the hospital where he was being treated. When the mob marched into Grant's jail cell, he said he didn't kill the chief—right before they killed him with three shots. The papers showed no sympathy for Bryan and Grant, only lamenting the death of Chief Freeman. If Bryan or Grant were my child, I would definitely have cause to curse the place responsible for their unjust murders.

When I asked her about the curse again, Mama said she doesn't believe the curse is real because she's a Christian. I think she doesn't want to be portrayed as superstitious to the public. I was recording an interview with her for a project. But I know what I saw flash in her eyes the day she first mentioned it: belief. Belief in a source of power beyond the confines of Christianity. Belief in a magic we thought got left behind in the home of our ancestors but has never really left us. Mama didn't mention being a Christian when she first brought up the curse. She recounted the story in the same tone as she would tell me the sky is blue. I heard not a trace of doubt. She felt comfortable in that chair, where her faith in the mystical slipped out of her mouth. Similar to the time she told me and Jojo over Olive Garden breadsticks she can see into the future. A part of Mama is willing to believe in other forms of spirituality besides Christianity—but she won't admit it on record.

Once upon a time in McIntosh County, there lived a beautiful young woman named Augusta. She walked to church with her little sister, Dee, nearly every Sunday of her life, but this Sunday was different. She looked the same as always: five foot six, slim with flawless sable skin, high cheekbones, pressed and curled shoulder-length hair, donning a tasteful, moderately priced dress from Sears. The pair took the same route along Highway 99 from their aunt and uncle's house to the church less than a mile away. Yet, that spring morning in 1957, the two young ladies moved slower thanks to a new addition to their party: Augusta's infant boy, Roy, already developing a reputation in the family for being headstrong.

At nineteen, Augusta knew the congregation would smile in their faces, then gossip about them around their supper tables. It sickened her that her innocent baby boy would be judged due to the purported sins of his mother. You see, Augusta wasn't married. She wished the fellow dwellers of Meridian, a tiny fishing village, understood dating was one of the only things preventing her from going stir-crazy. She envied the increasing number of local Negroes trading in the quiet hopelessness of McIntosh for the hustle and bustle of New York City. In NYC, there were work opportunities outside of white people's homes, and Roy could attend integrated schools with more resources than McIntosh's segregated Todd Grant School. Hopefully, NYC would be an option for Augusta one day…but not today. Today, she was broke and single with a brand new baby in a community where the Baptist church reigned and judged, then judged some more.

Taking a deep breath, Augusta stepped into the church building with Roy swaddled on her shoulder sleeping peacefully. She and Dee had barely settled onto their usual pew to the left of the altar when she felt a tap on her shoulder. She turned around to see Sister Parker, one of the ushers, beckoning her toward the vestibule. Augusta handed the baby to Dee and followed Sis. Parker, who placed her plump hand on the small of Augusta's back and guided her outside.

Sis. Parker took both of Augusta's hands into hers, looked her in the eyes, and said, "You know our church loves you and your precious baby boy, but we can't condone unwed mothers in *His* house. I'm afraid that you and your baby are gonna have to leave."

"I understand, ma'am," Augusta responded, never breaking eye contact with Sis. Parker's dark brown eyes in her round face.

"God bless you, Augusta."

"You, too, ma'am."

Augusta reentered the church, collected her baby and baby sister, and walked out the door with her shoulders pushed back, head held high. She wouldn't let them church people see her break a sweat, no sir. She asked Dee to carry Roy while she smoked a cigarette, reaching for the green pack of Salems in her pocketbook. She secretly pretended to be strutting down a packed sidewalk in Harlem instead of a desolate swath of grass and dirt.

Augusta would never live in Harlem, but she did make it to a nearby neighborhood in the Bronx. Shortly after being kicked out of her home church, she met and married Paul, a young man from nearby Savannah who often visited his relatives in Meridian. A pregnant Augusta waved good-bye to Paul as he enlisted in the Army. His service took him to the Middle East, where someone took a sepia portrait of him wearing the ghutra on his head, a white head covering folded into a triangle and secured with a thick black cord. After experiencing a mental break, the Army sent Paul to a psychiatric hospital back home, from where he instructed Augusta to name their baby girl Sue. They were eventually reunited, but Paul's failing mental health ruined their relationship. After their divorce, Augusta found herself alone in McIntosh with two young children and few prospects. Tired of scraping by as a domestic and short order cook, she made a tough decision. She needed to get out of the South to support her kids and have a meaningful life. Her mother would take care of the children for now while she tried to find work in NYC. She would lodge with a family friend in the South Bronx.

Augusta used her last dollars to board a segregated train car to NYC with one suitcase. Time passed quickly as she daydreamed of the father she never knew—a pullman porter shot and killed by a stranger in Savannah. Had he ever worked on this train? She tried not to feel intimidated when she arrived at Grand Central Station, blocking out throngs of people as she navigated her way on the subway to her new home in the Bronx. She soon found work as a hospital certified nursing assistant. Augusta felt proud sending *real* money home to her family. She loved smoking on her fire escape while watching shenanigans on the street, the music, parties, flirting, and fighting. There were Black people, Puerto Ricans and a sprinkling of white Jews. She tried to understand Spanish and Yiddish from context clues. You didn't hear loud salsa music or see yarmulkes where she came from.

Eventually, Augusta got her own place and sent for her daughter, Sue, my mother. Augusta got married to an unscrupulous man from the Caribbean at some point but was never really open about it (even though I did wonder why she would warn us randomly about Caribbean men). Meanwhile, teenage Sue and her girlfriends sometimes hung out at the park at night, watching rap battles and breakdancers. At almost eighteen, she married her first husband, a boy from McIntosh she'd known her whole life, in her family's living room. He wore an Afro, she wore white over her growing belly. Augusta smiled proudly in the wedding photos as Sue shyly grinned. Sue gave birth to my oldest sister, Renee, shortly after. A divorce and a second husband followed, yielding my sister, Nicole, then me, then another divorce.

Both Mama and Grandma migrated back to coastal Georgia in the late 1980s, an era of drugs and decay where they lived in the South Bronx. They wanted a slower, safer life for Renee and Nicole—and for me in my mama's belly—landing in Brunswick, the slightly more metropolitan city just south of Darien, along with other family members. Most of them joined a large, historic Black Baptist church in downtown Brunswick, where I got christened toward the end of 1987. About a decade later, for reasons I don't know and am wary to ask, Mama and Grandma drifted to Grandma's home church in Meridian, where we still had relatives. Most of the church elders probably knew about Grandma's unceremonious exit but acted as if they had forgiven her sins. When I got baptized there in 1997 at age nine, I had no idea Grandma had been expelled from its premises. If I had known, I imagine I would feel just as indignant about the incident as I do today. I already had a strong sense of justice. But I wouldn't have dared oppose my baptism because children didn't make their own spiritual decisions in my family. I would have swallowed my anger.

Upon returning to her home church, Grandma established a monthly birthday celebration like the one at her former church in Brunswick. She attended the church even as her lung cancer metastasized and ultimately killed her in summer 2006. Her funeral was held there, and she's buried less than two miles away from the church. I mostly forgive the church for their antiquated rules back then but can't help but hold on to a tad of resentment. If they could turn her away from their doors, surely, they would have shunned Mary Magdalene. Their behavior was *not* what Jesus would have done, not as I understood Jesus from the very stories they taught me. Sometimes I wonder what traditions we would have had if white slave masters had never introduced Christianity to the Black people they held in bondage. Their Bible taught enslaved Africans to oppress and subjugate their women, and the resulting patriarchy still dominates the Black Church. These beliefs hurt women like Grandma and LGBTQIA+ folks like me. Where or whom might we worship today had white Christianity not been forced upon us? What blessings—or curses—would we hold?

Fifty years after Grandma got forced out of her church, I had my own encounter with ungodly behavior from a self-proclaimed Christian in McIntosh. During my summer vacation from college, before most cell phones had a GPS app, I was driving my little brother and a family friend to a cousin's wedding deep in the woods of McIntosh and decided to pull into a grocery store to figure out directions. On one of Darien's main thoroughfares, I sped up to pass the driver in the right lane, an old white man, so I wouldn't miss my turn.

I parked in the store lot and was attempting to get internet service on my Motorola Razr when my brother pointed to the old white man standing next to my car. The man signaled for me to roll down my window.

After I obliged, he gruffly said, "You better be glad I'm a Christian with the move you pulled just a minute ago, missy."

He stalled for a minute for effect, then returned to his vehicle. Shaken up, I continued my journey. I wondered how a Christian could act like that. I had identified as a Christian since being Baptized. Nicole and I joined our church's children's choir for a short time despite rarely attending practice. We praise danced with other girls at church on Easter to Kirk Franklin's "Now Behold the Lamb." Most of my friends at school were also Christians. I went to their churches' youth groups, and nearly every Sunday in the summer, we went to the Gathering Place, a huge gathering of Christian youth in nearby St. Simons Island. During middle school and high school, I joined a Christian group called Y-Club, Fellowship of Christian Athletes, and Braveheart, a Christian sexual abstinence organization for teens. I got my first job the summer after ninth grade counseling teens over the phone at Braveheart. Me and a few girlfriends were in a Christian Bible study group my senior year where we met once a week at 7:07 a.m. with an adult leader, usually at Chick-Fil-A.

Grandma nor Mama shoved Christianity down my throat. No sermons. The two women were fairly devout but knew how to have a good time—more of the world than of the church. Mama drank alcohol occasionally. Grandma drank and smoked. Pieces of their lives clearly contradicted the Bible. We stopped going to church as much in my high school years, but Mama threatened to make me go with Grandma when I talked back or "caught an attitude." Nonetheless, it seemed like my Baptism had worked. I proudly identified as a Christian, even writing about trusting Him in my LiveJournal. I never got expelled nor suspended from school, only a few silent lunches and after school detentions. I had immersed myself in extracurricular activities and graduated high school with honors.

Setting off for the University of Georgia in August 2005, I had a strong Christian foundation. But church took a backseat to the thrill of queer parties and clubs and hungry kisses with girls in downtown Athens. Hundreds of miles away from home, I could be the real me, after nearly a decade of secretly lusting after girls. I blossomed as a bisexual feminist. In women's studies courses, I learned there are no gods, only prophets, in Black feminism. The Combahee River Collective taught me none of us are free until Black women are free "since our freedom would necessitate the destruction of all systems of oppression." Black feminism taught me to place belief in my own power, the power of Black women, and the power of social justice.

Black lesbian feminists of the past emboldened me to come clean about my queerness to my family. If Audre Lorde could do it in the 1960s, surely I could, too. I wanted to be brave like her. My sister, Nicole, was one of the first family members I told when I started dating my first girlfriend, K, in 2010. Nicole hinted to Mama one of her kids might be gay. I wasn't present, but my sister said she balked at the sheer notion. Mama deduced Nicole must be talking about me. She didn't cut me off when I told her about my first girlfriend or about Jojo. She first met Jojo in 2012 at Nicole's Fourth of July cookout, where she slyly asked to be introduced to my "friend." Mama quickly warmed up to Jojo but still reminded me whenever the spirit hit her:

The Bible says homosexuality is wrong. We had always had our differences, but my queerness drove the wedge between us deeper. The pain of her words slowly pushed me away from the Baptist church.

When I first moved to Durham, North Carolina, in August 2010, I tried out a Unitarian Universalist (UU) church. I liked the idea of believing something at the intersection of a lot of different faiths. On my first visit, I sat in a circle of chairs with a small, racially diverse group as the director of the Pauli Murray Center for History and Social Justice presented on Pauli Murray's life (1910-1985) in lieu of a sermon. I had never heard of Pauli before but immediately felt a kinship with them: Durham native, author, poet, pioneer legal scholar on gender discrimination or "Jane Crow," the first Black woman-identified person to be ordained as an Episcopal priest, good friend of Eleanor Roosevelt's, and a queer, gender-expansive person struggling to understand why God put them in a woman's body.

Years later, I read Pauli's family memoir, *Proud Shoes: The Story of An American Family* (1956), and their posthumously published *Song in a Weary Throat: Memoir of An American Pilgrimage* (1987). Pauli spent their entire life fighting to belong. Sent to jail in Virginia in 1940 for refusing to sit in the back of the bus. Petitioned for admission to University of North Carolina-Chapel Hill's graduate school and got denied due to their race, despite descending from one of the university's first trustees (Pauli had Black, white, and Indigenous ancestry). Only woman in her class at Howard Law. Fought to attend Harvard Law after receiving a fellowship as top law graduate but got denied due to their perceived gender. Pauli fought to fulfill their potential in a world where they were never meant to survive. I see myself in them.

Unlike me, Pauli leaned into organized religion. It comforted them after their partner died, especially since they had bonded over their faith. The Episcopal church elevated Pauli to sainthood in 2012. Saint

Pauli—one of my most important trans ancestors. I call their name whenever I can. (Around New Year's Eve 2021, for the first time, I walked the front yard of the home where Pauli's grandparents and aunt raised them as if it were hallowed ground.) The presentation at the UU church definitely intrigued me. Afterwards, I agreed to get lunch with some fellow church goers at an Indian place. I attended the church a few more times, as well as a local Metropolitan Community Church (MCC), a queer and trans-affirming denomination. A Black trans man pastored the church, bigger than the other one and also racially diverse. At the MCC church, I enjoyed hugs from strangers, feeling a warm hand on my shoulder, watching a praise dance that reminded me of home.

I stopped searching for a church home because I had life to deal with. I was severely depressed and could barely pay my bills. After K instigated our breakup, I became a fixture at downtown Chapel Hill bars and clubs, and house parties in Carrboro. I hooked up with more people than ever and drank and smoked weed more than ever. I was late to work nearly every day. At the beginning of 2011, I spent a few days in a psych ward and got evicted from my apartment that December. The next year, while unemployed for six months, I crashed on a daybed in Nicole's suburban Atlanta home, then on a futon in Renee's apartment near the Yankees stadium. I got interviewed then rejected from a retail job at Home Depot (I had easily secured a retail job the summer after high school).

Despite being a star student my entire life and graduating cum laude from college, I had still ended up a failure. I felt like I didn't have much of a future. I stopped believing in God because I prayed and prayed, but He forgot to answer. To this day, I can't reconcile Christianity with all the hate it causes in the world. Christian white supremacy rose with the presidential election of Donald Trump.

Because of Christians, people are losing access to abortions, trans people's lives are in danger, and K-12 schools are banning books about Black, brown, and LGBTQIA+ people. Christians are cursing us through their tried and true political action, oppression, lying, and cheating. I'm in no rush to be affiliated with these actions.

While I don't believe in Jesus anymore, I do believe in Saint Pauli, Mama Audre, Black feminism, and womanism. I believe our ancestors' spirits stay alive as long as we speak their names and honor their memories. When we remember our ancestors, they draw on their powers from the other side to make sure we're okay. That's why I keep reminders of Grandma, Aunt Nettie, and other deceased loved ones on the small white bookcase turned altar I share with Jojo. Its shelves are adorned with mementos and magic: photos, drawings, stones, plants, herbs, trinkets, and sacrifices, including egg shells, a can of lima beans, and a pack of fruit snacks.

I believe my family never fully lost our West African spiritual traditions. Mama and the Black mother who cursed Darien are part of an abundant lineage of African rootworkers.

At our church in Meridian, a spirit caused worshippers to clap and jump uncontrollably to the organ, keyboard, tambourine, and drums, roll their eyes to the back of their head, fall to the floor, and pass out. I saw it after folks gave their testimony on Watch Night (an African American New Year's Eve tradition) and during the altar call at the end of service when people would get "saved" and give their lives to Christ.

This spirit could only be traced back to our African origins—Europeans couldn't teach us how to praise like that.

Matthew Raiford working at Gilliard Farms, his family's ancestral farm in Brunswick, Georgia.

Reclamation

I CAN'T IMAGINE LEAVING GILLIARD FARMS IN Brunswick, Georgia, my hometown, uninspired.

In March 2022, I first visited the ancestral land of the Gilliard family. My spouse, Jojo, and I were in town for the inaugural Drapetomania Conference founded by the cultural preservationist Helen Ladson to combat local social injustices. I met Helen through my reporting on toxic industrial pollution in Brunswick. She invited us to a dinner after a full day of community discussions and door knocking. Among other dishes, we ate hay-smoked meat and sweet potatoes outside at a long picnic table. We were all Black, eight adults, two children, sitting under gigantic mossy trees on a farm tended by seven generations of one Gullah Geechee family since 1874. Gullah Geechee is a term I heard as a child. But I didn't understand until later the term describes the descendants of enslaved West Africans who live in insulated communities along the United States' coast between Jacksonville, North Carolina, and St. Augustine, Florida. The Gullah Geechee created arts, culture, language, and spirituality derived from their African homelands.

Most of the dinner guests were strangers to me, but we agreed the moment felt like time travel as we ate the food prepared and grown by two of the farm's owner-operators, Matthew Raiford and his wife, Tia Raiford. Matthew is the great-great-great-grandson of Jupiter Gilliard, a former enslaved person who in the 1870s amassed four hundred-seventy-four acres in the freedmen community of Brookman, a rarity during a time when most Black people share-cropped. Raiford's children are the seventh generation of the family to cultivate the land and reap its harvest.

Gilliard gave most of his land to extended family before he died, passing on forty acres to his two sons. In 2011, Matthew's great-aunt Ophelia (Gilliard's great-granddaughter), who he knew as Nana, deeded twelve acres of that land to him and his sister, Althea Raiford. After decades of traveling the world, including ten years in the Army, Matthew returned home to embrace his ancestral duty of tilling the land alongside Althea, a Navy veteran also returning to the land. One year in, the state awarded Gilliard Farms the designation of Centennial Family Farm, only the tenth Black farm to receive the honor. By then, the farm had already become one of the first to be certified organic in the state. Today, fifty-one-year-old Althea helps operate the farm from her home in the Atlanta area, while fifty-five-year-old Matthew takes care of day to day things on the farm with Tia.

"I am the prodigal son who returned, only with my arms wide open for the land I thought I had left behind," writes the "CheFarmer" (a term he coined to combine chef and farmer), author, griot, and food advocate in his 2021 cookbook, *Bress 'n' Nyam: Gullah Geechee Recipes from a Sixth-Generation Farmer*, co-authored with Amy Paige Condon. "Bress 'n' nyam" means "bless and eat" in the Gullah Geechee language.

At the dinner, mosquitoes swarmed, chickens clucked, kunekune pigs grunted. The scent of lavender wafted through the air. Kids giggled as they played on tree swings. I knew I wanted to write about this place one day. Matthew, a deep brown-skinned man wearing red glasses with the back of his head shaved and long locs pulled back in a thick braid, told us in his clear, rich tone how his ancestors practiced the same regenerative organic agriculture as he does today. This includes using pieces of plants and vegetables to grow new ones, composting organics to feed the soil, growing crops without irrigation, and never using chemicals.

He also spoke of similarities between African American and Indigenous American agriculture, recalling how his family burning leaves and spreading the ash on the ground to fertilize the soil is akin to Indigenous Americans' slash-and-burn technique. It almost feels like the two groups met *before* the transatlantic slave trade, one guest said.

We were joined by a few of Matthew's cousins who had recently migrated from up north to settle back on the family land. We sat a few steps away from Union School, a one-level retrofitted blue house with a screened-in front porch and a metal roof. Now occupied by Matthew's seventy-eight-year-old mother, it used to be the only school Black children could attend within a twenty-five-mile-radius serving grades K-8 from 1907 to 1955. Goosebumps crept up one of his cousin's arms as she stood where her father once stood as a young pupil. She felt as if she were transported back in time.

Being on the farm made me feel proud of being "country," a label I had been running away from since leaving Brunswick for college in Athens, Georgia, five hours away from home. Black kids were encouraged by our elders to leave the small city by the ocean as soon as we could, calling it too country and backwards. After graduating from college in 2009, I lived in Durham, North Carolina; Dallas, Texas and Seattle, Washington before settling back in Atlanta with my spouse in 2018. Around that time, I became fiercely protective of Brunswick while reporting on the disproportionately high amount of toxic chemical sites in its Black neighborhoods. I looked beyond the town's air and water pollution, and rampant racial inequities, to discover gems like Gilliard Farms.

Here are Black people in my own hometown doing the same work as their ancestors and my ancestors, too. Most descendants of enslaved Africans can trace our families back to roots that are rural, Southern, and connected to food. Both my maternal grandmother and great-grandmother were chefs in McIntosh County just north of Brunswick. In McIntosh at the Meridian dock, my family members "headed" shrimp in the mid-twentieth century across the water from Sapelo Island where the Geechee are now defending their land from the "good ol' boys," who want to use it to build expensive beachfront properties. My paternal grandmother picked cotton and other crops in rural eastern North Carolina. Yes, my ancestors lived off the land and sea, sustaining them for centuries. Yes, it's something to be proud of.

So I wonder what would happen if we descendants of enslaved Africans stopped running from the land and water from which our ancestors found survival?

What if we run toward reclamation instead?

What if we can potentially heal ourselves, our descendants, and our land by reaching back to our forebears?

What if Gilliard Farms is a glimpse of an Afrofuture where Black people's relationship to food and land is regenerative instead of fraught?

What if time traveling can save our lives?

Matthew grew up being disparaged about his roots, his country ways, but came to appreciate the descriptor when he got older. He told me other Black people, young and old, sometimes ask him why he's doing "slave work." People who don't know Black farmers are surprised to know they even exist—but Black farmers have always existed.

"My sister, Althea, and I have both had people say to us, 'Y'all going home to do that slave work?' What do you mean by slave work? Because we're going back to grow food so that you can eat. I'm not sure that's slave work," Raiford said. "Even when we were still in Africa, we farmed. We were engineers, technologically driven. We built things not through the direction of some colonizer but through the direction of the lens of where we were."

Matthew is no stranger to building things and has lived many lifetimes in one. Youngest boy in the family who came up in the kitchen. Desert Storm veteran. Culinary Institute of America graduate. Executive chef at upscale spots. Professor and culinary program coordinator. As the owner and operator of The Farmer and The Larder, a now-closed restaurant in downtown Brunswick, he earned a 2018 semifinalist nomination for a James Beard award, the food world's equivalent of the Oscars.

Building and rebuilding also applies to Matthew and Tia's love story. They first dated twenty-five years ago in culinary school when neither one of them had their mind on farming. They parted ways in 1998. Then, one of Tia's social media photos caught Matthew's eye in 2020, sparking a rekindling of their flame. Tia—the daughter of a musician father and a mother who grows food—had also lived many lives and traveled around the world, including working in Beijing, China, as a senior executive chef at the 2008 Summer Olympics and creating culturally relevant culinary programs for Philadelphia schoolchildren.

Tia is a toffee-colored woman who wears glasses and often a scarf tied around her hair like a headband. Despite being two generations removed from Alabama landowners and sharecroppers on both sides of her family, Tia spent most of her life in Northern cities before marrying Matthew. Alongside millions of other Black Americans, her parents' families moved up north for better job opportunities and better protections from racial violence in the mid-twentieth century. While digging into her genealogy, the fifty-year-old discovered Brunswick-Glynn County to be the birthplace of her paternal great-great-great-grandfather, Bill McDonald, born in 1820.

Gilliard Farms symbolizes a homecoming for Tia, who also identifies as a CheFarmer in addition to being a food educator and yoga teacher.

"To have lived this experience of knowing where my family comes from, being disconnected from the land through no fault of mine, and ultimately coming back south to do this work makes everything come full circle," she told me.

Now the duo spends their days running a business, Strong Roots 9 (honoring the nine dollars in taxes Gilliard paid on his land in 1874), a wellness omni brand of products for Black and brown skin; holding events at the farm like their annual "Pig Pikn'"; cooking at events across the country, like AfroTech in Austin, Texas; creating value added products like their Gullah Geechee Gin (they grow hibiscus and have it distilled and bottled by Simple Man Distillery); and of course stewarding their ancestral land, which now spans nearly forty acres.

Life on the farm comes naturally to Tia, even though she's never lived on one before. Both she and Matthew say she knows how to get things done on the farm instinctually. For instance, Tia always knows what to do with the chickens even though she's never raised chickens. She believes farming is embedded in the genes of all Black Americans.

"It's important for Black Americans to embrace this work because it's in our DNA. This is where we come from. We were and continue to be farmers, creators, and developers," Tia said. "We have not been given the opportunity in many instances to hold onto the land or tell the story of what it is to live on the land."

The Raifords see it as their responsibility to share knowledge with and advocate for Black farmers, who have dwindled in number over the past century because of intentional disinvestment and land theft. Only 1.4 percent of farmers in the U.S. today are Black, a staggering decline from fourteen percent one hundred years ago when there were nearly one million Black farmers. According to a 2022 study, Black farmers lost three hundred twenty-six billion dollars in land between 1920 and 1997. African Americans have been systematically locked out of land and home ownership. Historically, we couldn't get loans for homes in Black neighborhoods due to the racist practice of redlining, and racial covenants kept us from buying in white neighborhoods. Black people were some of the first to lose their homes during the Great Recession, when predatory lending caused millions of foreclosures and evictions. The United States Department of Agriculture (USDA) has *never* resourced Black farmers like they should. Case in point, only thirty-six percent of the Black farmers who applied for a USDA direct loan in 2022 got it approved, while seventy-two percent of white farmers were approved, according to a NPR analysis of government data. While interviewing folks for a story at a USDA press conference in 2021, I met people who believe they were entitled to settlement monies from the 1999 *Pigford v. Glickman* lawsuit filed by Black farmers against the agency to compensate for discriminatory lending practices but never saw a dime.

Now Black and brown farmers are suing the federal government for failing to deliver $4 billion in USDA debt relief promised to them by Secretary of Agriculture Tom Vilsack at that same press conference.

Given these sobering statistics, no wonder folks are surprised when meeting a Black farmer. We've been told Black Americans don't farm when our ancestors were stolen from Africa precisely for our agricultural prowess. Many of our ancestors purchased land during Reconstruction only to be displaced during the era of Jim Crow. We've lost Black farmers in the U.S. at such a rapid pace because they've been stripped of their power via land loss.

As Matthew likes to say, "Land is power."

The systematic dispossession of Black land, including in their own family, drives the Raifords' advocacy for African American farmers: They're currently raising funds to buy twelve acres on the farm a relative got manipulated into selling twenty years ago. Matthew speaks up for the specific needs of the state's Black farmers as board chair of the nonprofit Georgia Organics. "I've had people say things to me like, 'Why are you only pushing on Black farmers?' And I say, 'It's because Black farmers haven't been talked about.' The *Pigford* case is why we need to continue having this conversation," he said. "I meet Black people all the time who say, 'My grandparents left one hundred acres, and my aunts and them are trying to figure out what to do with it.' My response is always, 'Lease it to a Black farmer.' I say this because I personally know a lot of Black farmers who are landless."

Matthew doesn't think all Black Americans need to farm—but there are several factors pointing to why we should at least know where our food comes from and which plants and animals we can survive on in cases of emergency. We should at least consider *why* we can't grow food ourselves. The volatile climate of both politics and the environment threaten our ability to access food. Due to the

COVID-19 pandemic, we've experienced the dread of facing near empty grocery stores. Food issues arising from the pandemic include what to do when stores run out of groceries and how to eat when ordered to shelter in place. Now is the time for us who don't farm to locate the growers in our communities.

"Everyone should know or have contact with a farmer so they can understand what it takes to get the food on their plate," Matthew said.

On the road to reclaiming our ancestors' culture, Black people across the diaspora must unpack and dispel myths about who we are. For centuries, either others have dictated to us who we are, or we've been told we have no culture at all. The Raifords are big on the power of telling our stories and wielding them to preserve Black culture.

"We need to be loud about our voice and what our accomplishments are so that that recognition is not getting whitewashed, stolen, watered down, or mocked. I think it's critical. We have thousands of years of stories to tell that have been erased," Tia said. "Now we're an oral culture. However, there were deliberate decisions made to make sure our history was not traceable. It's time for us to be able to tell our story in our own voice."

A lot of our culture has been spoon-fed to us, Matthew said, but he's started to see a shift in the past fifteen years, with technology playing a major role in that. His storytelling praxis is grounded in both ancient and new modes of communication. He tells the story of Jupiter Gilliard over and over again so it hopefully never gets lost. His descendants won't have to go on a wild goose chase to find out who and where they come from.

"When we let someone else tell the story about us, we get stuck in their perspective. I always want to be able to talk about my story and my family's story. I want my kids to be able to tell the story of their great-great-great-great-grandfather and all of the people who came after and before," he said.

The couple is also collaborating with Ladson and her nonprofit, Heritage Works, that empowers Brunswick's Gullah Geechee residents to draw from their cultural heritage to gain economic self-sufficiency in one of the area's largest industries, tourism and hospitality, by training to become docents, construction workers, or culinary artists (a third of residents in the majority-Black town live in poverty). The Raifords are spearheading the nonprofit's culinary track.

"Gilliard Farms has been so gracious with their land. Matthew and Tia have made it very clear they want their farm to be used for the uplift of the community. They've made it their business to make sure community events are happening on the farm and people feel welcome," said Ladson, who is also Strong Roots 9's chief joy officer. "The role they play [at Heritage Works] is the same role they play everywhere, which is being hospitable and giving people."

Strong Roots 9's motto is "Honor the Past, Grow the Future." The Raifords are harnessing their farm's resources to build toward an Afrofuture where Black people know where our food comes from and honor farming as an integral part of our history and culture. Their plans include scaling up Strong Roots 9 production, building farm stays on their property, holding solstice and equinox dinners, and partnering with companies to buy their crops. They plan to preserve the schoolhouse and sugarcane press. They hope to be a model of self-sufficiency and to advocate for community control of our food system. Ultimately, they envision the farm serving the community as an educational center where you can learn how to farm and how wellness is connected to what you eat.

*

I returned to Gillard Farms in October 2022 for a weekend-long conversation about Black culture keeping. There were ten in our group. We kicked off the weekend with a Friday morning tour of the farm led by Matthew, beginning near a bottle tree meant to ward off evil spirits in Gullah Geechee culture. At home as a storyteller, Matthew instructed us to close our eyes and imagine what it was like there one hundred years ago before cars and highways, when Black children walked for miles to get to Union School. We toyed with the boundaries of time as he guided us, connecting the past to the present while sharing aspirations for the future. Ushering us through the farm, Matthew pulled up plants with his gloved hands for us to smell and taste, asking if we could identify them (I mostly couldn't).

The farm pulsed and buzzed with life. A coop filled with chickens soon to be plucked, dressed, and sold through a CSA (community supported agriculture). Pastel eggs soon to be sold, too. Five spotted pigs native to New Zealand. A teaching area where they experiment with crops dedicated to Nana who switched up what she grew yearly. Mint planted above the ground to keep it from growing wild. Plant medicine everywhere: milk thistle, turmeric, aloe, lemon balm, lemon grass, ginger, rosemary, oregano. Figs, beautyberries, Persian limes, and Santa Rosa plums fruiting on trees. Burdock root next to motherwort, olive trees next to parsley and basil because they grow well together. Cayenne peppers and jalapenos. White amaranth to keep pests away.

I saw closeup what regenerative organic agriculture looks like. They cut the stems of scallions, dry them, and put them back in the ground to grow new ones. They grow new sweet potatoes from the sprouts of old ones. Everything from oyster shells to fish bones is composted and broken down by black soldier flies. These methods are even older than the sugarcane press brought to the farm by Matthew's great-grandfather in 1919. Yet these methods still work because our ancestors knew what they were doing. They knew how to grow and cook good food. They knew how to keep themselves healthy.

Take potlikker for instance, the liquid left over after cooking down collards, a forever favorite in African American families. Matthew, who not only grows collards but is also researching them as a Mellon visiting scholar at the New York Botanical Garden, says drinking pot likker is good for fighting colds and resetting gut health. He said he plans to write a cookbook to include, alongside recipes, how the name "colewort" transmuted to "collards" over time and the historical relationship between collards and Blackness.

"We've been eating right. We came over here with that knowledge. Then we're told, 'Pot likker? You must be poor.' No, I must be healthy. Poor ain't in it. Healthy is in it."

Mama poses for a picture with Neesha in her arms at their aunt's home in McIntosh County, Georgia, Christmas Day 1987.

Stealing Sheetrock

"HAVE YOU EVER HEARD OF A BOOK CALLED *PRAYING for Sheetrock?*" I asked my mother on my pink Motorola Razr while sitting in my residence hall's computer lab.

I'd been assigned the 1991 nonfiction book by Melissa Fay Greene in my Georgia history class at the University of Georgia. A few pages into my hardback copy, I realized it was set in McIntosh County. I doubted the majority of my classmates, mostly white kids from Atlanta suburbs, knew where to locate it on a map: tucked in a southeastern pocket of Georgia alongside the Atlantic. I was born and raised in Glynn County, directly south of McIntosh, where my mother and her mother were raised. On Sunday mornings, my siblings and I would pile into Mama's Honda Accord dressed in our finest garb, as she drove us twenty miles north on Highway 17 to her family's religious home, the Baptist church in a McIntosh community, Meridian. After, we congregated at my great-aunt and her family's home down the street from church where we would eat heaps of food. Meridian made where we lived, the small city of Brunswick, look like a bustling metropolis. I felt bored driving past the endless creeks, rivers, marshes, pine and live oak trees, churches, and rickety trailers of McIntosh. I dreamed of one day living in a big city like Atlanta or New York. I never anticipated having my roots thrust into my face by a white history teaching assistant.

"The one with the people on the highway picking up shoes?" Mama questioned in response to my query.

That was the one. She was referring to the book's prologue, in which Greene describes the aftermath of two trucks crashing on Highway 17 in Eulonia, an all-Black hamlet nine miles north of Meridian, in June 1971. With McIntosh County Sheriff Tom Poppell presiding over the scene, Eulonia residents helped themselves to fancy, brand new leather shoes spilled out onto the highway by one of the trucks, greeting a silent Poppell while doing so. Greene casts Poppell as villain of this story. The sheriff's appearance didn't necessarily project power a white, white-haired, five foot nine, one hundred fifty pound-frame clad in the fashion of the day (think bell-bottom slacks and white loafers)—but his commanding aura was legendary.

The author writes that the sheriff represented the last of the "good ol' boy system": white male political bosses who governed their municipalities with an iron fist through corrupt behavior. Illegal gambling, prostitution, and speed traps were all permissible on his watch as long as he got a cut of the loot. Back then, every Black person in McIntosh was registered to vote, and they always voted for Poppell—or else. According to Greene, Black folks in McIntosh respected him because he knew them all by name and would look out for them, like keeping his mouth shut as they indulged in spilled goods on the highway, a frequent occurrence. She writes that they revered the "High Sheriff" despite his role in keeping them so poor one of them prays for sheet-rock to finish building her home. Poppell made sure they didn't have access to good jobs or housing. Black and white citizens alike feared this dictator who had the last say on all local affairs, but white folks knew they would be punished less severely than their "Negro" counterparts for their trespasses.

"Well, you can tell your professor that Mother used to cook for the sheriff," Mama said as we chatted about the book.

Mother is what we called my maternal great-grandmother who died when I was in eighth grade. Before asking Mama about *Praying for Sheetrock*, I'd never even thought about what Mother did for a living. She was retired by the time I came around in 1987. Turns out, in addition to operating a beauty salon out of her home in Darien, McIntosh's county seat, Mother cooked for the notorious Sheriff Poppell. I can picture Mother, a stout, blue-black lady who wore a wig, confidently clanging pots around a humid kitchen to prepare Poppell's food. The image is jarring since I rarely even saw her in the vicinity of a white man. Mother sat at the head of our dinner table and at the front of our church. She was a proud woman, the leader of our family, and a leader at church. I hope she held her head high as she served that skinny white bigot, even if she feared his power. Mama says Mother would yell at my uncle for fighting white kids who taunted them because she was afraid the Ku Klux Klan would burn down their home. Perhaps Poppell helped instill that fear in her.

Greene portrays the Black community of McIntosh as docile, gullible, and unworldly. "At the time of the shoe truck in 1971, the black community of McIntosh County was blind and deaf to issues of civil equality, equal employment, and local corruption," she writes in her prologue. During my recent reread, I couldn't help but question Greene's reliability as narrator of this story. I question whether a white Jewish woman raised in Ohio who stumbled across McIntosh while working with the Georgia Legal Services Program can shed her inherent biases when interviewing Southern Black folks. I read an article online where she says her interview subjects perceived her as a fellow outsider, and she regarded them as friends. I would never depict a friend as helpless as Greene paints her subjects to be.

The author frames the election of Thurnell Alston, a Black retired boilermaker and former union steward, to the McIntosh County Commission in the 1970s as the catalyst that finally ushers in the Civil Rights Movement (she characterizes Alston as an unlikely leader because of his stuttering, high-pitched voice). There is no mention of Tunis Campbell, a Black man originally from the Northeast who held several leadership positions in McIntosh and the state of Georgia in the 1860s. In March 1865, Campbell was appointed by the Freedmen's Bureau to help resettle land on five of Georgia's sea islands. He bought 1,250 acres of land in McIntosh and established a settlement of Black landowners called Belle Ville. He served as state senator, president of the state Republican Party, and delegate to the state constitutional convention. As retribution for executing the aims of Reconstruction, Campbell was terrorized by the KKK. His family lived in fear like my great-grandmother did a century later. Still, local Black people didn't take the terror sitting down: Three hundred of them once defended Campbell's home from the KKK. In a similar turn in 1899, hundreds of Darien's Black residents guarded the city jail with arms to stop a white lynch mob from getting to Henry Delegale, a Black man falsely accused of raping a white woman.

Where are these acts of Black rebellion in Greene's narrative? In a review essay of *Praying for Sheetrock*, historian James E. Goodman expresses confusion over Greene's omission of Black people's post-emancipation struggle in McIntosh: "That is so obvious an oversight that I repeatedly found myself paging backwards to see if there were sentences or paragraphs I missed." I can't help but wonder if Greene commits historical erasure to serve her sleepy and subservient depiction of my ancestors.

Greene waxes poetically about McIntosh's Scottish roots but rushes through a description of the "Gullah language" as a blend of "English, Scottish, and African tongues" that formed in McIntosh's Black community due to their isolation (I've never read anywhere else about the language having Scottish roots). In doing so, she disregards the rich, unique ways of life of the Geechee people in coastal Georgia (the Geechee live in Georgia and Florida, the Gullah in the Carolinas). Gullah Geechee isn't just a language—it's an entire culture that also includes arts, crafts, food, spirituality, and music. Green proffers the "Gullah language" as a symbol of lack instead of the asset more and more people are realizing it to be. Today, even the National Parks Service is invested in preserving this culture, designating the land along the coast from Jacksonville, North Carolina, to Jacksonville, Florida, as a "National Heritage Area." And Gullah Geechee are being featured more often in mainstream media. So much for Greene's "unworldly" label.

Greene assumes the African Americans of McIntosh lack culture. She assumes McIntosh remained segregated until the 1970s, more than a decade after Brown v. Board of Education, because white people wanted it that way. She assumes Black people in Mcintosh wanted integration. But I remember riding in the car with Mama when I was ten, and her saying, "I went to a segregated school, and they should've kept things that way. We were happier back then." She would get angry at me for having so many white friends. When I first wanted to go on a date with a Chinese boy, Steven, the summer before tenth grade, she got frustrated.

Steven was in the grade above me, and we didn't share any classes, so I didn't know him well in real life. I don't even remember how I became friends with him on MSN Messenger, but before I knew it, I was chatting with him late into the night. He would tell me how fine he thought I was, and when I flipped my yearbook to his picture, I liked what I saw. A cutie with spiky hair and a gold chain. A JV football player with a brain, enrolled in advanced classes. I loved being the center of his attention. He kept asking to take me out, but I was scared to ask my mom. I had never gone on a date with a boy alone. When I went to the Homecoming dance and to the movies with a date, friends had always accompanied us. Plus, although Mama knew I'd had boyfriends before, they had all been Black.

One Saturday summer afternoon, I worked up the nerve to ask Mama if the boy could pick me up for us to go to Chick-fil-A. Butterflies cocooned in my stomach as I took a deep breath and walked to her bedroom, where she was watching TV from bed.

"Can I go to Chick-fil-A with a boy from school? His name is Steven, and he has a car, so he can pick me up.... Erin can come, too, so we won't be alone." Erin, a white girl, had been one of my best friends since sixth grade.

Mama sat up with a stern look in her eyes.

"I don't know this guy. I don't know his parents. Why should I let you go with him? Is he even Black?" I think she suspected Steven might be white since Erin was.

"No...he's Chinese."

"I'm not letting you go out with some Chinese boy who I don't know. Dammit, why don't you have any Black friends?" she yelled before slamming her bedroom door.

She reacted like I thought she would. Before the end of the summer, she consented to me going out with Steven, as long as friends came with us. She still wished I had more Black friends and would have probably been more accepting of Steven if he were Black. She perceived anyone who wasn't Black as a potential enemy. I thought Mama was old-fashioned and a tad ignorant, but as an adult, I'm better able to place myself in her shoes. She was in fifth grade when the white kids invaded the all-Black school she knew and loved, and they didn't come in peace. She must've felt like I do when white people intrude into all-Black movement-building spaces: like something sacred has been breached. On ancestry.com, I discovered a yearbook photo of Mama taken shortly after the integration of Mcintosh schools. She wears a plaid collared shirt, hoop earrings, ear-length relaxed hair parted down the middle, and a hesitant smile. She looks like she doesn't know how to be happy in the middle of racial turmoil. To Greene, integration signaled promise, but for Mama, it marked the end of life as she knew it.

Shortly after that photo was taken, Mama went to live in NYC with her mother who moved there in the 1960s because she couldn't find work in McIntosh except for "heading" shrimps at the docks, working as a short order cook, and working in white people's homes. Up north, Grandma found work as a certified nursing assistant at a hospital. She didn't have time to wait around for McIntosh to change because she had a family to feed. Black people in McIntosh were self-sufficient—fishing, farming, and hunting for their families and their livelihoods—until they couldn't be anymore thanks to capitalism, industrialization, and speculative development. Greene often references how white residents called Black residents, who comprised most of the county, "the sleeping giant." I don't think Black folks in McIntosh opted out of the Civil Rights Movement because they were sleepy and simple. I think they were being worked to the bone by white people for poverty wages, taking care of their families, and going to church instead.

In the second part of Greene's book, the author writes about the police shooting of a Black man named Ed Finch in March 1972 as the "awakening" that propels Thurnell Alston into running for the county commission. Darien's white police chief, Guy Hutchinson, saw and heard Finch and his girlfriend fussing with each other at her place across from the city jail. When Finch refused to quiet down at Hutchinson's request, the Archie Bunker look-alike shot a .38 caliber revolver into Finch's mouth, then stuck him in the jail-house without medical attention as blood spewed out of his mouth. The incident was too egregious to ignore for the Black people of McIntosh, who appointed Alston as their de facto leader. Dressed in their Sunday's best, three hundred Black residents from all over McIntosh descended upon Darien's city hall armed with guns and a list of demands, including for Finch to receive immediate medical care and for the police chief to be suspended.

When city officials acquiesced to their demands, the Black community marinated in the taste of collective power. A series of organizing meetings hybridized with revivals ensued in the county's Black churches. Greene presents the "Three Musketeers," Alston and two other Black men, Nathaniel Grovner (a minister and educator) and Sammie Pinkney (a retired NYC cop), as the ring leaders of change. The three establish the McIntosh County Civic Improvement Organization, a local NAACP chapter, and work with the Georgia Legal Services Program to file lawsuits against McIntosh and the city of Darien, winning more Black representation on the grand jury that selected the Board of Education and increased Black voting power through redistricting. After years of running, Alston is finally elected

to the county commission in 1978. Black men had served in the position before him, but they'd been handpicked by Poppell to be figure-
heads, not to actually represent the Black community's interests.

Alston's commissioner position eventually wears him down and
renders him disillusioned; he feels as if he's carrying the entire Black
community's burdens without their support. The book ends with
the death of Poppell in 1979, and Alston being sentenced to seven-
ty-eight months in prison for making a cocaine deal with an under-
cover Georgia Bureau of Investigation agent in 1987. Finch, whose
shooting by the police chief started the uprising, was charged with
aggravated assault and obstructing an officer immediately upon being
released from the hospital. He was indicted on both counts by an
all-white jury, served six months in jail before being paroled, and
was shot to death in Texas in 1976 (the book doesn't say who killed
him). Hutchinson got his police chief job back less than a month after
shooting Finch.

The state of civil rights in McIntosh today does not exactly inspire.
Driving through the county in recent years, it looks the exact same
as it did during my childhood. The 2020 U.S. Census Bureau indicates that it's no longer majority-Black. On their county commission,
there is one Black person out of five members. Many residents have
forgotten about Alston and Greene's book. The people who Greene
interviewed have mostly passed. The good ol' boy system the author
claims died with Poppell is still in full effect in coastal Georgia, as
evidenced by the February 2020 murder of a twenty-five-year-old
Black man named Ahmaud Arbery in Brunswick by three white men,
including one of my former classmates, Travis McMichael. Arbery, a
former high school athlete with family roots in McIntosh, was simply jogging through a neighborhood when the men cornered, shot,
and killed him. The district attorney, a white woman named Jackie

Johnson, didn't arrest the three men until three months later when a video of the killing went viral—likely because of her relationship with Travis' father, Greg McMichael, who had been a former investigator in her office. Johnson perpetuated the good ol' boy system without even being a "boy." (A criminal case against Johnson for meddling with prosecution has been delayed since March 2023.)

The McMichaels and their accomplice, William "Roddie" Bryan, originally pleaded "not guilty" to all charges. The murder of Arbery has sparked a movement much like the one in Greene's book, including the emergence of new racial justice organizations, a campaign to remove a Confederate monument from a public park that won, and the successful passage of a state hate crime law. My heart aches for Arbery's family, who will never truly get justice because he can't be brought back to life. At least his family got more reparations than most. They wanted his murderers locked up for good, and that's what they got. After the Arbery family opposed the McMichaels' plea deal to serve thirty years in federal prison in exchange for guilty pleas, the district judge rejected the agreement. In January 2022, the McMichaels were sentenced to life in prison without the possibility of parole. Their accomplice, Bryan, got life in prison and won't be considered for parole for thirty years. The following month, the three men received federal charges for interference with rights (a hate crime) and attempted kidnapping, with the McMichaels receiving an additional charge for using a firearm during a violent crime. The power of the people led to this outcome, not the benevolence of the judicial-legal system in coastal Georgia, which is still corrupt and white supremacist.

How many more iterations of the same movement must we have before oppressive systems change for good? I believe feeding the prison industrial complex and calling for police reforms only begets more oppression. There is no way to reform an institution rooted in keeping African Americans enslaved and stealing their labor. Prisons are no harbinger of justice. I would be lying, however, if I said the imprisonment of Arbery's murderers didn't feel a little like progress compared to what happened to Finch.

Today, Greene lives with her criminal defense attorney husband in Atlanta and has a boatload of children and grandchildren. She has published a total of six books, contributed to periodicals such as the *New York Times* and *The Atlantic*, and is the Kirk Distinguished Writer-in-Residence at Agnes Scott College. *Praying for Sheetrock*, her debut book, was a finalist for the National Book Award.

When I ask myself whether Greene had a right to tell this story, the answer is different every time. *Praying for Sheetrock* is undoubtedly well-written and contains a wealth of knowledge, but it also overlooks the important history of Black resistance in McIntosh. Currently, it's being turned into a feature film, and I'm afraid that it, too, will omit this truth. If I could have my way, a Black person with ties to McIntosh would direct it. That's who I want to translate my ancestors' freedom struggles onto the screen. Otherwise, I'm not sure the movie will do right by them. Their story deserves to be told with the utmost care and respect.

If I were the director, I would add the Darien Insurrection of 1899 to Greene's narrative. Imagine it: The date is August 21, the sun is scorching, and the air is muggy. A well-known, local Black man is arrested upon being accused of rape by a white woman who just gave birth to a mixed-race baby. Henry Delegale is incarcerated, even though neither Black nor white residents believe the woman due to her poor reputation. The sheriff announces he wants to transport Delegale to Savannah for "safekeeping," but Black townspeople know that means he will be lynched while en route. Their mission: to stop the man from being removed from the jail by the sheriff.

Overnight, Delegale's sons mobilize a hundred armed Black residents (some sources say hundreds) from throughout McIntosh to guard the Darien jail, to ensure Delegale won't be lynched. For the next two days, each time the sheriff attempts to remove Delegale, designated watchmen ring the bell of a nearby Black Baptist church for Black residents to assemble and defend the jail. The sheriff asks the governor to send in the state militia. On August 24, the insurrectionists are arrested. When two white "temporarily appointed deputies" are dispatched on August 25 to the Delegales' home to arrest Henry's sons for inciting a riot, one of the deputies is shot and killed and the other severely injured. The Delegale matriarch pleads with troops to protect her family from the sheriff and his posse, who are on their way. Miraculously, the troops convince the posse to stand down. The *Savannah Press* publishes this headline about the events on August 26: "RACE WAR IMMINENT; TROUBLE NOT ENDED."

The race war envisioned by white folks never ensues. The commander of the state militia meets with ten prominent Black male leaders who publish a circular asking Black residents to refrain from "inciting white violence." They direct the circular toward Black men, the heads of their households, asking every Black man to stand down and to "see to it that no colored woman shall show her face at the courthouse or on the streets thereto."

Henry Delegale lives to see his day in court, where he is exonerated. Two of his sons are given a life sentence for shooting the deputies and killing one of them, while two of Delegale's other children are acquitted. Forty of the rioters' cases are dropped, and the other twenty-three are convicted and sentenced to perform hard labor and pay fines. In violation of convict release law, two women are sentenced to work on a sawmill. The outcome of the insurrection isn't exactly just, but it also isn't catastrophic as it could've been.

Ultimately, the insurrection paid off. It prevented the lynching of an innocent Black man—proof that McIntosh's Black population knew how to fight white supremacy long before Greene claims they did.

Neesha smiles for a photo, circa 1996.

16

Facts of a Black Girl's Life

Sixty-seven percent of Black girls report having been touched, grabbed, or pinched in a sexual way at school.
American Association of University Women

I LEARNED BOYS FELT ENTITLED TO MY BODY IN fourth grade. At only nine, almost a B cup, my breasts were budding much faster than my peers'. I excitedly bought my first bras at Walmart.

At school, I shared a desk with George, a skinny Black boy with a raspy voice. Boys and girls weren't typically friends unless they were "talking," so I rarely interacted with him. I felt ambivalent about George until the day he socked me in the breasts. It was the first time I hated my body. Ashamed, I folded my arms over the bear hugging a heart on my T-shirt, over my chest.

227

That's when I started to feel like I had to accept unwanted touch into my life. I've never shared any of this with anyone because society has conditioned Black girls to believe no one cares what men and boys do to our bodies.

Black girls are viewed as less innocent and more adult-like than their white peers.
Georgetown Law

As a teen, I didn't think of myself as attractive. For years, I'd been teased about my wandering right eye, big forehead, and flat affect. By eighth grade, I also had big boobs, a small waist, a flat tummy, and long legs. These assets garnered attention from boys—and also middle-aged men, including my eighth grade science teacher, Mr. Lieberman. A graying white man with glasses and fuzzy brows, he often strayed from the curriculum with random stories, including one about his long friendship with a phone sales lady. I excelled in his class and won awards for having the highest grade.

I never had a problem with Mr. Lieberman—his class was pleasant enough—until the day he touched me.

While cranking the pencil sharpener's handle, I felt fingers softly tracing the back of my shoulders and my shoulder blades. I turned around, and there stood Mr. Lieberman wearing a straight, serious face. We locked eyes for a moment, and then I walked back to my seat. I laid my head on my arms and prayed nobody had noticed. I treated the incident like a bad dream, shoved it out of my memory. Reporting him to a principal or guidance counselor never occurred to me. I ran into him a few years later while accompanying my little brother to a countywide sports event. There with his daughter, Mr. Lieberman said he spotted me from across the room.

"I knew it was you because of your cute purse," he said, pointing to my pink monogram Dooney & Bourke. I feel nauseated when I consider the possibility of his comment being a double entendre.

Ninth grade, it was Señor Smith, a red-faced man with dirty blonde hair who had taught my sister a few years before. I made all 100s in his Spanish I class, earning the nickname "Estrella" or "Star." I rarely received affirmations at home, so I ate up his compliments. Señor Smith laid them on thick. On a fill in the blank exam question calling for the conjugation of the irregular verb "ser" or "to be," I noticed the subjects of the sentence shared the exact same first names as me and my sister. It said we were "chicas hermosas" or "pretty girls." I couldn't decide whether to be flattered or embarrassed. This confusion returned one morning as a friend and I walked back to Señor Smith's class from a school assembly. The teacher stood by his classroom door, smiling, hand rubbing his chin, eyes burning holes into my turtleneck sweater and jeans.

"Where do you and your sister get your looks from?" he asked me.

I mumbled something about my mother. Sliding into my desk, I drowned in worries. Is this what womanhood felt like? Had my girlhood come to a premature end?

Thirty-eight percent of students in grades eight through eleven report being sexually harassed by teachers or school employees. American Association of University Women

＊

Mr. Lewis, my eleventh-grade trigonometry teacher, also adultified me. Another white middle-aged man, he replaced one of the few Black teachers at my school. She had made me sit up a little straighter, try a little harder. Once Mr. Lewis took over spring semester, I swiftly lost motivation. I missed a test and made it up in his classroom one day as he ate lunch. My eyes glazed over at the equations, and I verbalized my confusion. Mr. Lewis welcomed the opportunity to come sit down beside me, close enough to touch me. He grabbed my pencil and completed the problems for me. I nearly gagged at his tuna breath creeping down my V-neck shirt, but I didn't move away from him. He was enjoying coming to my rescue. After that, any time trig confused me, Mr. Lewis saved the day. I rewarded him by allowing him to invade my space.

For most of my high school career, I helped design and edit a literary magazine we published each spring. During class, Mr. Lewis agreed to buy a copy from me but said he needed to fetch the money from his car.

"Come with me," he beckoned.

Face ablaze, I followed him out the classroom door. I could feel my classmates staring at us. We walked side by side, my fingertips grazing my bare thighs underneath gym shorts. It was early afternoon, and the weather was sunny and perfect, nowhere near as oppressively hot as it gets during a coastal Georgia summer. The fresh air did nothing to cool my face. We ended up at an outdated sedan, what you would expect an underpaid teacher to drive. Mr. Lewis sat in the driver's seat while I stood right outside of it. He turned on the cassette player.

"This is no orrrdinary love, no orrrdinary loveee," Sade crooned to soft music.

Mr. Lewis smiled up at me. "You like that?"

I laughed nervously. Mr. Lewis placed a five-dollar bill in my hand,

and we headed back to the classroom. I placed one shaky foot in front of the next.

On the last day of school, I laughed nervously, again, as he held his arms out to me in his empty classroom. I felt like I couldn't decline his hug since I had welcomed the closeness between us. I blamed myself for his antics.

In twelfth grade, Mr. Simmons didn't give me a chance to deny his affection. A gray-haired white man with a big belly and Coke bottle glasses, he handled my high school's printing needs and taught my literary magazine class alongside Ms. Christian, a young blonde who wore lots of black. He typically sat in his corner desk as Ms. Christian led the class, his eyes engrossed in his computer screen.

During my senior year when we were tasked with selling useless items for a fundraiser, Mr. Simmons agreed to buy from me. Standing beside his desk, I graced him with a dimpled smile and words of gratitude. Mr. Simmons responded by pulling me into a hug and planting a kiss on my cheek. A familiar heat crept from the pit of my gut to my face. I told my friends about the kiss but of course never thought to alert an adult.

Out of every one thousand sexual assaults, nine hundred-seventy five perpetrators will walk free.
Rape, Abuse & Incest National Network

I came of age in the early 2000s. We didn't talk openly about sexual assault and harassment like we do today. We didn't have a #MeToo movement. Nobody ever taught me about consent. Nobody acknowledged our rape culture. We lived in a climate where super predators like R. Kelly evaded accountability despite outrageous evidence. Folks acted as if the man who sang "I Believe I Can Fly" could do no wrong, especially in Black American families like mine. A tape of R. Kelly peeing on a girl younger than me leaked during my ninth-grade year on the same day as his performance at the 2002 Winter Olympics. A month later, he released an album with Jay-Z, debuting at number two on the Billboard 200 chart. The summer after ninth grade, he got indicted on twenty-one counts for the acts caught on tape, but the survivor refused to testify against him, so all the charges were dropped.

At Thanksgiving dinner my eleventh-grade year, several times, Mama requested for the young people to dance to R. Kelly's new, feel-good song, "Step in the Name of Love (Remix)," inspired by a Chicago dance style. We all happily obliged, prancing around the living room as the singer proudly proclaimed to be the "Pied Piper of R&B." I viewed R. Kelly as perverted for urinating on young girls, but no one else seemed to be bothered by it. So, I grinded to the remix to "Ignition" at school dances alongside everybody else.

R. Kelly's survivors have only recently begun to receive some semblance of justice. It took two decades and an entire Lifetime series to get to this place. Shortly after he was convicted on nine counts of sex trafficking and racketeering in 2021, I sat on my couch watching a YouTube video of one of the survivors who testified against him, Azriel Clary, being interviewed by Gayle King.

The video flashed back to one of Gayle interviewing Azriel a year before. Twenty-one-year-old Azriel barked at Gayle about how happy she was with R. Kelly, who was more than thirty years her senior, while covered up to her neck in all-black. She said her parents were lying about their relationship to the media to scam him. She threw a tantrum while a young woman in red to her left rubbed her back, R. Kelly's other girlfriend. Gayle alerted viewers the singer was lurking in the shadows during the interview. Then, the video flashed back to the new interview with Azriel wearing a formfitting outfit, looking happy and confident while bearing bags underneath her eyes like battle scars. She admitted R. Kelly coached her and his other girlfriend to be angry and upset with Gayle before the first interview. She spoke about how she endured R. Kelly's physical and verbal abuse from age seventeen and how everyone around them normalized it. Nobody could've gotten her to leave, she said. It's a lesson she had to learn herself.

"I was lost, I felt invisible, and I gave someone that control over me to make me do whatever it was that they wanted me to do and act however they wanted me to act," Azriel explained.

Putting R. Kelly behind bars brought the light back to Azriel's eyes. Watching the video, I silently cheered for the young woman. I felt as if she were my little sister. I saw myself reflected in her. As a prison abolitionist, I don't believe incarceration will truly rehabilitate the R&B superstar nor heal his trauma of being sexually abused as a child. I wish our society had real alternatives to the prison industrial complex, an inhumane remnant of chattel slavery. Yet I feel relieved to know R. Kelly no longer has unfettered access to Black girls and women. It's better than him facing no consequences at all, which is too often the case.

Recovery from sexual violence is facilitated by social support.
Research in Nursing and Health

Collectively, my run-ins with teachers made me feel like my body no longer belonged to me. I felt powerless and perplexed. Authority figures thought they had a right to access my body and sexuality at a time when I was just discovering who I was. I accepted their bad behavior as an aggravating but normal part of life. I think that's why I liked having a boyfriend in high school and college: Guys were less likely to harass me with a dude by my side. I felt like I had a protector. But when I went out scantily clad to the club with girlfriends, I accepted unwanted hands on my body because I thought I had "asked for it" with the way I was dressed. I felt powerless in my early twenties during incidents like driving south on I-16 with a man driving right beside me, smiling and jacking off, and later receiving an unsolicited "dick pic" from a guy I met randomly at a NYC pizza joint. When I told a family member about the latter, her response was, "Well, was it big?"

Her reply is indicative of how sexual harassment was treated in our culture before the #MeToo awakening: like some big joke. Today, trans and queer-only spaces feel safer to me than being around cisgender heterosexual men. Sexual violence absolutely happens in LGBTQIA+ communities, but the difference is most of us weren't raised to feel entitled to other people's bodies. Thus, we're more likely to practice consent. I feel lucky to have been exposed to consent culture through my friendships with other queer and trans people.

A confused teen no more, I envision a world where Black women, girls, and femmes are protected from all forms of violence as a writer and community and cultural organizer. I imagine a world where Black girls are safe at school and everywhere else. I report on how fellow queer and trans people of color are responding to intimate partner violence in our communities. I helped organize a Black Womxn Matter event in 2016 with music, poetry, and an altar adorned with the names and photos of murdered Black trans women. Around the same time, my spouse and I supported a group of young women who successfully got a middle-aged activist with a twenty-year history of objectifying young women fired from his youth organizing job. We made sure they knew his sexual harassment wasn't their fault.

While supporting survivors of sexual violence, I grew to accept the actions of George and my teachers were never my fault. I did nothing to deserve unsolicited hands on my body nor unsolicited eyes on my chest. Writing this is part of my healing journey, as is confiding to my therapist, spouse, and sometimes even X/Twitter followers. Each day, I tend to the hurt child inside of me like a flower. I sing and write to her. I encourage her self-expression. I work to make her feel whole and worthy of protection. I work to make her feel less alone.

I hope my seven nieces will never have to experience their own George, Mr. Lieberman, Señor Smith, Mr. Lewis, nor Mr. Simmons. I want them to know they aren't just another statistic. I also want them to know their body belongs to them alone, that others need to ask for permission to touch it, and that it's okay to tell folks "no." If they receive unwanted touch, I hope they feel empowered to alert the appropriate person and to speak out if their case isn't treated fairly. And if they enter romantic relationships, I hope they get to share their bodies on their own terms.

Aunt Nettie's nieces: Renee holding her baby sister, Neesha, circa 1987.

Dancing in the Wind

GAZING OUT THE CAR WINDOW, I OBSERVED THE contrast between the carefree children on the school playground and the cemetery parallel to it where a few dozen somber people gathered to bid farewell to Aunt Nettie. The kids must've been used to the sight of a funeral procession, but that didn't stop them from staring at the cop car leading Aunt Nettie's body to its final resting place and the hearse and two limos behind it.

Aunt Nettie was going home. Her home. She was returning to Jesus, who she praised her entire life in choir stands and liturgical dances. She posted a Bible verse on Facebook daily, all the way up until she got admitted to the hospital for severe COVID-19 symptoms around Thanksgiving. I only talked to her once after that as she breathed with the help of a ventilator. "The good Lord don't make no mistakes," she assured me. She died a month later on Christmas Day. Her body was transported from Grand Blanc, Michigan, to her childhood home, Darien, Georgia, where she was to be buried next to her mother and father across from Todd Grant Elementary School, once a K-12 segregated school for local Black children from where she and several of my other relatives graduated.

Dressed in gray from head to toe, I sat in the back of the second limo, wedged between my oldest sister, Renee, and my wife, Jojo, and behind a cousin I hadn't seen in years and her husband, a man wearing a clerical collar who I'd just met for the first time. At the cemetery, we waited for the chauffeur to let us out but ended up letting ourselves out once it took him too long. I adjusted my N95 mask and the sunglasses my sister Nicole insisted I wear. "It's our *thing*," she had said. There was plenty of sun to block out despite the weather being in the fifties, unseasonably cold for coastal Georgia in January. I took my place at the back of a short line with my sisters and Jojo to view Aunt Nettie's body lying in a white casket under a canopy tent.

Once we got to the front, Nicole linked arms with me to steady herself, her stilettos sinking into the red earth. Our mother, not in attendance because she was taking care of another ailing aunt, had seen pictures from Aunt Nettie's wake the day before. "She doesn't look like herself," she lamented over the phone. I couldn't make an accurate assessment, given I hadn't seen my great-aunt in-person in almost a decade. She wore a matronly black wig in her casket—I preferred the fun gray curls she sported in her most recent Facebook photos. At least she looked peaceful. I wanted to touch her, but I refrained from doing so. Nobody else was touching her, and I stupidly wondered if I could catch COVID-19 from her corpse.

Silently, I asked Aunt Nettie for forgiveness. I'm not like her; I don't know what I believe happens to our souls after we die. I don't know if our spirits stick beside the people who loved us when we were alive. I like to think my ancestors are protecting me, which is why I showcase their photos on an altar, but I'm honestly not sure if there's an afterlife at all. Wherever Aunt Nettie was, I hoped she could hear my silent plea. She had wanted to come to Atlanta for Thanksgiving. "I need to see my family," she wrote to me on Facebook. I didn't offer her a bedroom at my place because Jojo and I were in the middle of a stressful move. My siblings didn't have room nor capacity to host her either. So, she planned to stay at a hotel, but she never made it down south. She landed in the hospital with COVID-19 instead. The guilt still eats away at me. Aunt Nettie had just entered her seventies. I should've made more of an effort to see her. The godmother who stayed up all night to sew my lace-adorned christening gown, slip, bonnet, and booties. The baby sister of my beloved grandmother. I should've asked to read her work from the bachelor's in English and creative writing program she completed well into her golden years. I should've let her know I still cared.

A few years prior, I tried to visit Aunt Nettie when I attended a conference in Detroit about an hour away from her home, but she declined, saying she was busy with chores, church, and work. I wrote her off then because of my fragile ego. She doesn't want to see me because I'm queer, I decided. I made it so her posts didn't show up on my Facebook newsfeed. I found her constant prayers and Bible quotes to be excessive. I couldn't shake the hurt of her not dropping everything to visit with me in Michigan, so I looked at them as hypocritical. She loved God, Jesus, and the Holy Ghost enough to center them in her life, I thought to myself, but she didn't love me enough to fit me into her busy schedule. I forgot about the good times we shared. They came flooding back as soon as I received the news of her death on Christmas morning.

One of my fondest memories with Aunt Nettie is the time we rode together to Atlanta in her little red car for a church trip, while Mama and Grandma rode on the church bus. I chomped on Twizzlers and read my newest *Baby-Sitters Club* book as she took long sips from a jug of water. I was nine in fourth grade, newly admitted into my county's gifted program.

"How many Black kids are there in your gifted class?" she asked.

Just me, I answered.

"Do you think that means white kids are smarter than Black kids?"

I don't remember what I answered, but her questions stuck with me. They went above my head then, but she was trying to get me to think about how racial inequities manifest in privileged spaces. Mama nor Grandma never asked me such questions. I knew Mama didn't care for race mixing, but I chalked this up to her being a dinosaur stuck in the days of segregation. Aunt Nettie subtly contextualized institutional racism for me in a way no other adult ever had simply by asking questions that forced me to think about being the only Black kid in the room. Most folks I knew in real life and on TV pretended we were living in a post-racial society, like racism was a thing of the past. This exchange with Aunt Nettie percolated in my brain a few days later when we visited a church in Forsyth County on the outskirts of Atlanta, infamously featured on *Oprah* for keeping Black residents out up until the early 1990s.

During that same trip, while sitting on a church pew next to Mama and Grandma, an official-looking man tapped me on the shoulder.

"Sister Nettie asked for your assistance."

Feeling important but bashful, I shuffled behind the man, who showed me to a room where Aunt Nettie was getting ready for her praise dance performance. I helped zip up her dress and fasten the buttons on her sleeves. She handed me a set of flags that I placed at the center of the stage before she went on, then skittered back to my seat. Brimming with satisfaction, I watched my tall, yellow-skinned aunt beam and twirl in her flowy white dress, feeling like her right hand man. She could've asked an adult to assist her, but she trusted little ol' me to get the job done.

Aunt Nettie had a knack for making me feel like I mattered. She bragged about me and my sisters' accomplishments to whoever would listen. Most adults treated me like a powerless kid, but she treated me like an autonomous being and encouraged me to think for myself. She'll never know what she meant to me because I couldn't swallow my pride, I thought, as I left her casket to sit underneath the tent next to my sisters and spouse. I read Aunt Nettie's funeral program as I waited for the service to begin. Usually, she oversaw making our family's funeral programs, and I wondered who would inherit her role. She looked angelic in all white in the cover photo taken during one of her dance performances, even wearing a wreath around her head. My name made it into the program as her sole godchild. "This is going on our altar," I told Jojo.

A man from the funeral home closed the casket before the service began, topping it with a bouquet of yellow flowers. The same pastors who did Grandma's funeral, back when we took being packed in a church without masks for granted, officiated over Aunt Nettie's funeral. Each gust of wind made me hug myself tight, but my discomfort was nothing compared to the importance of paying my last respects to my godmother. My cousin's husband who we rode in the limo with read Psalm 23. They should've asked me to read it, I thought. Rev. Mims spoke about how as a child, Aunt Nettie had been her personal angel who warded off bullies on the school bus. A young woman who I didn't know with a lovely voice sang "I Won't Complain" by Rev. Paul Jones. Looking at her bare legs made me shiver. One of my cousins sang two selections at a keyboard. First

Mahalia Jackson's "That's All Right," then one Aunt Nettie had performed to, "I Can Only Imagine," by MercyMe. I loved that song in high school before I renounced Christianity. The singer muses about what it will be like when it's his time to meet Jesus.

The man who baptized me but barely recognized me at the funeral, Rev. Jackson, made the final remarks. There were a few more lines in his face and a few more pounds on his frame, but otherwise the cocoa-colored pastor looked the exact same as when I was a child. His hair appeared chemically straightened into an S-pattern and a thin strip of hair graced his upper lip. He wore rectangular glasses, a prominent ring on each hand, and a black clergy robe. Rev. Jackson promised not to keep us too long on account of the cold. His statuesque wife stood close by, picking up stray papers the wind blew off his makeshift pulpit. He called Aunt Nettie a "showstopper" who filled the room up with her presence—somebody who wasn't perfect but loved the Lord in all she did.

Listening to his sermon felt surreal. I couldn't remember the last time I'd sat through the Word. I was so different from when I spent Sundays in the pews of Rev. Jackson's church. A small-town, straight Christian girl grew up to be a queer, non-binary Atlantan who believes in astrology, tarot cards, and ancestral worship in lieu of Christ. I began embracing alternative belief systems in my early twenties because I felt betrayed by Christianity but still needed a lens through which to make sense of the world. Mama kept using the Bible to justify why being queer was wrong. Hateful Christians were to blame for why I couldn't marry Jojo until we moved to Seattle in 2014. I knew all Christians didn't hate LGBTQIA+ people, that LGBTQIA+ Christians exist, and that queerphobes and transphobes have misinterpreted certain Bible passages to serve their interests. But I was tired of fighting for acceptance, which I'd been doing my entire life. It felt foolish to be part of an entity that questioned my humanity.

When I stopped being Christian, I filled the void with practices learned from other queer and trans people. My spouse and I own three amazing tarot decks: the New Orleans Voodoo Tarot, the Hoodoo Tarot, and the Next World Tarot. The former two pull from indigenous African cultures in the Americas, while the latter is grounded in social justice. Things I can believe in without feeling shunned. On the surface, I don't have much in common with the fourteenth-century Europeans who originally created the tarot nor the eighteenth-century Europeans who first used the cards for divination. Yet I feel a kinship with them rooted in creativity and searching for meaning in a mysteriously beautiful but heartbreaking world. I rarely find myself in Christian spaces, but when I do, I sit respectfully and quietly, like at Aunt Nettie's funeral. Although my mind wandered, I tried to look attentive as Rev. Jackson spoke, nodding and clapping at the appropriate times. My heart quickened when I heard him say, "The good Lord don't make no mistakes." Aunt Nettie's last words to me. I sat up a little straighter. Was my aunt speaking through him somehow?

The reverend asked us to stand. "Earth to earth, ashes to ashes, dust to dust," he recited. One by one, the flowers were removed from Aunt Nettie's casket in preparation for it to be lowered into the ground. We made our way back to the limo, which would transport us to an aunt's house nearby for the repast—just for family due to COVID-19 restrictions.

In the limo, Jojo turned toward me and my sister. "Did you notice the wind blowing during each of the songs?" Yep, Renee replied. Like a typical Gemini, I'd been too wrapped up in my thoughts to notice.

"That was Aunt Nettie dancing," Jojo said matter-of-factly.

If Aunt Nettie had indeed been at the funeral, that means she heard me ask for forgiveness. I know she would've had grace for me.

I wanted to believe what my wife said...so I did.

References

Berea College. "The Power of Sankofa: Know History." Accessed June 18, 2024. https://www.berea.edu/cgwc/the-power-of-sankofa/.

Best Places. "Zip 31327 (Sapelo Island, GA) People." Accessed June 18, 2024. https://www.bestplaces.net/people/zip-code/georgia/sapelo_island/31327.

Blake, John. "There's one epidemic we may never find a vaccine for: fear of black men in public spaces." CNN, May 27, 2020. https://www.cnn.com/2020/05/26/us/fear-black-men-blake/index.html.

Brundage, W. Fitzhugh. "The Darien 'Insurrection' of 1899: Black Protest During the Nadir of Race Relations." *The Georgia Historical Quarterly* 74, no. 2 (Summer 1990): 234-253. https://www.jstor.org/stable/40582867.

Bustillo, Ximena. "In 2022, Black farmers were persistently left behind from the USDA's loan system." NPR, February 19, 2023. https://www.npr.org/2023/02/19/1156851675/in-2022-black-farmers-were-persistently-left-behind-from-the-usdas-loan-system.

Celeste, Manoucheka. "Close-Up: Black Images Matter: 'What Now?': The Wailing Black Woman, Grief, and Difference." *Black Camera: An International Film Journal* 9, no. 2 (Spring 2018): 110–131. https://doi.org/10.2979/blackcamera.9.2.08.

DeGraft-Hanson, Kwesi. "Unearthing the Weeping Time: Savannah's Ten Broeck Race Course and 1859 Slave Sale." Southern Spaces, February 18, 2010. https://southernspaces.org/2010/unearthing-weeping-time-savannahs-ten-broeck-race-course-and-1859-slave-sale.

Epstein, Rebecca, Jamila J. Blake, and Thalia González. "Girlhood Interrupted: The Erasure of Black Girls' Childhood." Georgetown Center on Poverty and Inequality, June 27, 2017. https://genderjusticeandopportunity.georgetown.edu/wp-content/uploads/2020/06/girlhood-interrupted.pdf.

Georgia Women of Achievement. "Katie Hall Underwood." Accessed June 18, 2024. https://www.georgiawomen.org/katie-hall-underwood.

Goodman, James E. "Review: Stealing Sheetrock." *The Georgia Historical Quarterly* 76, no. 4 (Winter 1992): 872. https://www.jstor.org/stable/40582761.

Greene, Melissa Fay. *Praying for Sheetrock.* Da Capo Press, 1991.

Hedrick, Amy. "War Between the States: American Civil War, Glynn County, Georgia." GlynnGen.com Coastal Georgia Genealogy &

History, accessed February 25, 2022. http://www.glynngen.com/
military/civilwar/glynn/.

Hobbs, Larry. "Memories of Cusie and cleaning up some mistakes." The
Brunswick News, March 2, 2019. https://thebrunswicknews.com/
news/local_news/memories-of-cusie-and-cleaning-up-some-mistakes/
article_382fe01a-736e-5913-b57e-974d50c523d0.html.

Longley, Robert. "All About Relative Depravation and Depravation
Theory." ThoughtCo., August 3, 2021. https://www.thoughtco.com/
relative-deprivation-theory-4177591.

Lowcountry Digital History Initiative. "Enslaved and Freed African
Muslims: Spiritual Wayfarers in the South and Lowcountry."
Accessed March 10, 2022. https://ldhi.library.cofc.edu/exhib-
its/show/african-muslims-in-the-south/five-african-muslims/
salih-bilali-bilali-mohammed.

Mallett, Kandist. "The Response to the Capitol Riot Is Whitewashing
the History of Black Insurrection." *The New Republic*,
January 18, 2021. https://newrepublic.com/article/160962/
living-tradition-black-insurrection.

Martel, Heather. "Colonial Allure: Normal Homoeroticism and Sodomy
in French and Timucuan Encounters in Sixteenth-Century Florida."
Journal of the History of Sexuality 22, no. 1 (2013): 34-64.

McFetridge, Scott. "Black farmers sue government for promised federal
aid." PBS, December 6, 2022. https://www.pbs.org/newshour/politics/
black-farmers-sue-government-for-promised-federal-aid.

Merriam-Webster. "On the History of the 'Rolling Stone.'" Accessed March 5, 2022. https://www.merriam-webster.com/words-at-play/rolling-stone-phrase-origin.

Parker, Adam. "Lowcountry and Rwandan women weave 'sweetgrass baskets of peace.'" *The Post and Courier*, September 21, 2021. https://postandcourier.com/news/local_state_news/lowcountry-and-rwandan-women-weave-sweetgrass-baskets-of-peace/article_6f26aef6-1b02-11ec-b0c1-535a2edd6ca6.html.

Psychology Today. "Terror Management Theory." Accessed February 27, 2022. https://www.psychologytoday.com/us/basics/terror-management-theory.

Research from *The Brunswick News* articles scanned by Lori Hull, manager at the Brunswick-Glynn County Library

Simms, Renee. "For Crying Out Loud." *Guernica*, November 10, 2020. https://www.guernicamag.com/for-crying-out-loud/.

United States Zip Codes. "ZIP Code 31327 Map, Demographics, More for Sapelo Island, GA." Accessed June 10, 2024. https://www.united-stateszipcodes.org/31327/.

Note on Photography

Acknowledgments

I PROCRASTINATED WHEN IT CAME TO WRITING these acknowledgements. The mood never felt quite right. So much has shifted and changed personally and in the world since I started working on this book in 2020 while in graduate school. Being a Master of Fine Arts in Creative Writing student immersed in writing, reading, thinking, and learning feels almost like a dream. Now it's 2024, and I have little time for these activities; I feel a bit unequipped to conclude this lifelong dream of writing a book. But self-doubt be damned—here goes nothing:

Giving birth to *Come By Here: A Memoir in Essays from Georgia's Geechee Coast* has truly been a community effort. I'm listed as the sole author, but I couldn't have possibly achieved this on my own. Firstly, thank you to the team at Hub City Press (HCP) for taking a chance on a little-known Black queer author. Thanks to Katherine Webb for championing my writing since 2021; for connecting me with HCP; and for editing my manuscript with care, intention, and grace. Thanks to Meg Reid and Kate McMullen for helping guide me through the publishing process, and for running a press that values talented yet overlooked Southern writers from historically oppressed groups. Thanks to Julie Jarema for staying on top of all things marketing.

This book is a result of revising and expanding my MFA thesis, *Outsider: The History of a Life and a Place*. Thanks to the faculty of the MFA in Creative Writing program at Georgia College & State University for helping me get here, especially my thesis advisor, Dr. Chika Unigwe, and my first creative writing professor ever and thesis committee member, Dr. Kerry Neville. Both of you were unapologetically critical when my writing needed it and laudatory when my writing deserved it. Thanks to Dr. Stefanie Sevcik for your helpful feedback as my other thesis committee member. Thanks to classmates and colleagues who helped me survive graduate school during an unprecedented pandemic: Merick Alsobrooks, Moriah Bray, Dr. Irene Burgess, Chandra Cheatham, Megan Duffey, Avery James, Charlotte Lauer, Jessica McQuain, Kelli Piggott, Jennifer Watkins, and Shannon Yarbrough. Thanks to the Georgia College Office of Grants and Sponsored Projects for funding my MFA education.

Thank you to the following folks for so generously showing and teaching me what it means to preserve Gullah Geechee culture and history: Maurice Bailey, Hermina Glass-Hill, Helen Ladson, and Matthew and Tia Raiford. Thanks to A Better Glynn and Glynn Environmental Coalition for sharing your stories with me of working to make coastal Georgia a healthier and more just and equitable place to live.

Thank you to Press On, Fernland Studios, and Art Farm at Serenbe for dedicating resources to the completion of this book. Thanks to Jessica Lynne for your sharp feedback on my manuscript and to Tanaya Winder for your essential feedback on my essay, "September." Thanks to all the teachers who encouraged me to keep writing along the way, especially the late Valerie Boyd, my favorite journalism professor at the University of Georgia. Thanks to Michelle Zenarosa and Danielle Amir Jackson for being editors who believed in my work. Thanks to Lori Hull, manager of the Brunswick-Glynn County Library, for helping me locate news articles while researching for this book. Thanks to Charis Books & More, Highlander Research and Education Center, and KB Brookins for your eagerness in helping me promote this book. Thanks to the many people who've patronized my work over the years, especially my friends, Mariam Asad, Shaun Glaze, and Mavina Lim. Thanks to my supportive community of friends and comrades, especially the members of Queer The Land.

To my family: I know some parts of this book will be difficult for you to read. I want you to know I would never put my life on "front street" if I didn't think it might help someone else. I don't know of any other Black, queer, and disabled woman from coastal Georgia who has published a memoir. With this book, I'm striving to combat the erasure of people like me from the archives, let them know their stories matter, and maybe even inspire them to document their own lives. I sincerely regret if I misremembered or misrepresented any family stories.

Despite any differences we've had, you all have always supported my artistic endeavors. Mommy, as a single mother you prioritized enrolling me in dance classes, driving me to and from drama club meetings and performances, and bringing home empty notebooks from work for me to fill up with drawings and writings, among other efforts that nurtured my creativity. I will never be able to thank you enough. Thank you to Dannie for digging up old family photos. Thank you to my entire family for your support.

Last but never least, I'm deeply grateful for Aimée-Josiane, my life partner for the past twelve years. Thank you for believing in my writing when I didn't, for being my constant cheerleader, for holding me down during grad school and times of underemployment, and for giving me crucial feedback on my manuscript. The shape of our relationship may change, but my love and care for you are forever. Thank you for allowing me to share our story in these pages.

**HUB CITY
PRESS**

PUBLISHING
New & Extraordinary
VOICES FROM THE
AMERICAN SOUTH

FOUNDED IN Spartanburg, South Carolina in 1995, Hub City Press has emerged as the South's premier independent literary press. Hub City is interested in books with a strong sense of place and is committed to finding and spotlighting extraordinary new and unsung writers from the American South. Our curated list champions diverse authors and books that don't fit into the commercial or academic publishing landscape.

Funded by the National Endowment for the Arts, Hub City Press books have been widely praised and featured in *the New York Times, the Los Angeles Times, NPR, the San Francisco Chronicle, the Wall Street Journal, Entertainment Weekly, the Los Angeles Review of Books,* and many other outlets.

RECENT HUB CITY PRESS NONFICTION

All of Us Together in the End ✦ Matthew Vollmer
Landings: A Crooked Creek Farm Year ✦ Arwen Donahue
George Masa's Wild Vision ✦ Brent Martin

HUB CITY PRESS books are made possible through the generous support of grants and donations from corporations, state and federal grant programs, family foundations, and the many individuals who support our mission of building a more inclusive literary arts culture, in particular: Byron Morris and Deborah McAbee, Charles and Katherine Frazier, and Michel and Eliot Stone. Hub City Press gratefully acknowledges support from the National Endowment for the Arts, the Amazon Literary Partnership, the South Carolina Arts Commission, the Chapman Cultural Center, Spartanburg County Public Library, and the City of Spartanburg.

Adobe Jenson Pro 10.8 / 15.3